Vada Moore

Please

Return

THE COMPLETE
AUSTRALIAN CATTLE DOG

JOHN & MARY HOLMES

HOWELL BOOK HOUSE

New York

HOWELL BOOK HOUSE
A Simon & Schuster Macmillan company,
1633 Broadway, New York, NY 10019.

MACMILLAN is a registered trademark of Macmillan, Inc.

Library of Congress Cataloging-in-Publication data

Holmes, John, 1913–
    The complete Australian Cattle Dog/ by John and Mary Holmes

        p.   cm.
    ISBN 0-87605-014-3
    1. Australian Cattle Dog.   I. Holmes, Mary. II Title
    SF429.A77H65   1993
    636.7'3 – dc20   93-17877
                                                            CIP

10 9 8 7 6 5 4 3
Printed and bound in Singapore

CONTENTS

Photo by Sally Anne Thompson.

**This book is dedicated to Aust. Ch. Landmaster Darling
Red, 'Honey'. Our first ACD, and our best friend.**

ACKNOWLEDGEMENTS

It would have been almost impossible to write this book without help from knowledgeable ACD enthusiasts throughout the world. It is not possible to thank everyone individually, but we do sincerely thank everyone who has helped us with information and photographs. We apologise to those who sent photographs which we were unable to use.

Our special thanks to Sally Anne Thompson for the excellent photographs she took for this book; to Phil Tyler for the line drawings; to Meyrick Stephens and Dr Christopher May for their contributions; to Kent and Lori Herbel for their contribution on Stock Dog Trials; to Gayle Beer, without whose tireless and patient help this book would never have been written.

Our thanks also to Kent Lithgow, Lorraine Teston, Connie Redhead, Phil Morrison, Karin Schmidt, Marja Vornanen, Maggie Monical, Meaghan Thacker, and various Kennel Clubs for their help. No book on the ACD would be complete without reference to Robert Kaleski's *Australian Barkers & Biters*. We appreciate having been able to quote from Ms M. K. Balmain's fascimile reproduction.

INTRODUCTION

It was when we went to Australia in 1979 that we saw our first Australian Cattle Dogs. We had been sponsored to give talks on training to clubs around Adelaide, Melbourne, Canberra, Sydney and Tasmania, and we saw several of the breed at training classes which we attended. They were different from anything we had seen before, and we both found them rather fascinating. During our tour, we stayed for a time with a friend who had worked for us before emigrating and now lived near Adelaide.

She told us that Connie Redhead, one of the most successful breeders of ACDs in Australia, lived nearby, and we immediately arranged to go and see her at her Landmaster kennels. Here, we got quite a surprise when we saw ten or eleven puppies, from two litters, all running together in a large grass run. On asking if they were around eight weeks old, we were told that they were only five weeks! We realised then that the breed was different from any other we had so far met.

Connie had exported ACDs to the USA, Canada, and several European countries, and one of her ambitions was to be the first breeder to send one to the UK. She could not understand why no one in Britain had taken up the breed. This view was shared by the late Thelma Gray, a very old friend from Corgi days (she sold the British Royal family their first Corgis), who at that time was living near Adelaide. In fact, she wrote the Foreword for Connie's book, *The Good Looking Australian*. It was obvious that Connie regarded us as a means of realising her ambition, and she used her very best sales talk to persuade us to buy one of the very nice young bitches she had for sale. However, it was over twenty-five years since we had done any breeding or showing, and we had never even considered the possibility of importing a new breed.

Following our visit to the Landmaster kennels, we talked a lot about what we had seen; we tried to find out as much as we could about the breed, and the idea of having one of these dogs seemed to grow on us. So, before leaving for home we went back to see Connie, and to have a look at a young red bitch we had taken a liking to. She was by 'Sunny', the great Australian Ch. Landmaster U' Sundowner, who was in his heyday at that time and was obviously a dog of great character. The idea was to have her mated and tested in whelp to Aust. Ch. Landmaster Eureka, before leaving Australia.

However, the cost of the bitch was relatively unimportant compared with the cost of transport and quarantine once she reached England. We therefore decided to wait until we got home and had time to consider all the pros and cons, before coming to a final decision. Connie was absolutely delighted when we telephoned to say we had decided to have the bitch, and soon we were told that the bitch had been mated, and it was only a question of being patient, pending confirmation that she was in whelp.

But it was not to be. Connie rang to say that veterinary tests showed she was not pregnant. However, Connie was still very anxious that we should have the first ACD in the UK, and she offered us another young bitch, also by Sunny, and already tested in whelp to Eureka. She was already an Australian Champion, and she had done a lot of winning. Much to our surprise, Connie said we could have her for the same price. We had seen this bitch, but she was one of Connie's favourites, and definitely not for sale at the time, so we had not paid any particular attention to her. John rang Thelma Gray, who lived quite near to Connie, and asked her to go round and have a look. She rang back saying to buy her quickly – before Connie changed her mind!

So this was how we came to own Aust. Ch. Landmaster Darling Red ('Honey'), who duly arrived at Ryslip Quarantine Kennels, owned by Liz Cartledge and her late husband, Joe, both of whom were very good friends of ours. When it was announced in the dog papers that the first of the breed had arrived in this country, we had a telephone call from Malcolm Dudding in Kent. He told us he had two blue ACD pups in quarantine. So, in spite of her efforts, Connie did not export the first ACD to the UK – but Honey certainly went on to be a credit to her.

We visited Honey as often as we could spare the time, and we found her to be very friendly, and popular with the kennel staff, and after a few visits she was obviously delighted to see us. Then we had a telephone call from Jackie, the headgirl at the kennels, to say that Honey had whelped a litter of six puppies. "Are they all right?" we asked, "How is Honey?" Jackie replied: "Oh yes, they are lovely pups, and Honey is fine – but all the pups are white!" We had forgotten to inform the kennels that ACD puppies are always born white, with or without dark markings. Knowing the nature of the breed, we rather wondered if Honey was going to be a bit possessive about her pups, but we need not have worried. She was delighted to show them off, proudly, to anyone who was interested. She simply adored her puppies in this and in subsequent litters; and of course they were a great comfort to her during her solitary confinement in quarantine. In spite of all the care and attention which we knew she received, she, along with all the other dogs, were still prisoners doing a stretch of 'solitary'.

One of the most inexplicable rules of the British quarantine regulations is that puppies can be taken out of quarantine at eight weeks, provided they have been away from their dam for two weeks. The dam must still complete the full six months. This was very unfortunate for Honey, and we must admit it was something we had not thought about beforehand. Although she appeared to be all right in the kennels, when we took her out it was obvious that she was verging on a nervous breakdown. She barked continually; in fact, she croaked, as her voice had become hoarse. When we put her in a big grass run – something she hadn't seen for six months – she rushed continually from one end to the other, jumping up at the fence like a newly captured animal in a cage. We were very worried about her, and we felt guilty, thinking that we were the cause of her trauma.

However, Honey made a remarkable and speedy recovery. Quarantine affects different dogs in different ways, usually for the worse. Whether or not Honey was the same after she recovered from quarantine, as she was when she left Australia, we are not sure. She retained her croaky voice right to the end, but she was a great character, a remarkable brood bitch, and a much-loved and devoted companion to us both. I think we can honestly say that she had a very happy life with us in the UK.

Connie was genuinely fond of Honey, and she never lost interest in her. It was only because of our disappointment at the first bitch not being in whelp that she decided to sell her. But we feel sure that we are right in thinking that Connie is very proud of Honey's achievements in the UK. For our part, we shall always be grateful to her for letting us have a 'dog in a million'.

Chapter One

HISTORY OF THE BREED

ORIGINS OF THE ACD

The Australian Cattle Dog is a comparatively new breed; it is a manufactured breed, and a good deal has been written about its origins. This much we know; what we don't know is how much of the written information is accurate. Historians of all breeds of livestock usually overlook the fact that a pedigree is simply a piece of paper with a lot of names on it. Its accuracy depends entirely on the person who wrote it out. Breeders who were developing or improving a new breed or strain, were often very secretive about any new blood they were introducing.

John was once offered a Welsh Cob colt "with papers". He was typical of the breed, and a great mover. But he has a very good memory for animals, and remembered seeing this one as a foal with its mother – and she was a Hackney! People like John, brought up among breeders of pedigree livestock, know that this sort of thing has always taken place, although it has been greatly reduced in recent years with the advent of DNA genetic finger printing.

For much of what was written about the breed, we have to thank the late Robert Kaleski. Born in 1877, he started breeding ACDs when he was sixteen and continued to breed, work and show them until his death in 1961, at the age of eighty-four, when he still had ten ACDs in his kennels. He was also a journalist who contributed to a number of agricultural and other magazines, and it was he who drew up the first Standard of the breed, in 1903. This was accepted by the Kennel Club of New South Wales the following year, and is very similar to the Standard still used by the Australian National Kennel Council. Robert Kaleski wrote a book entitled *Australian Barkers and Biters*, which was published in 1914, and covered many different breeds. It appears that this met with a certain amount of criticism when it was first published, and in the light of up-to-date knowledge, many of his theories are quite ridiculous. But so far as the origin of the ACD was concerned, he was dealing with fact rather than theory. Many of the original breeders would still have been alive when Kaleski was writing about them, so he would still have had access to first-hand information. Anyhow, it is largely due to his writings that much more is known about the origins of the ACD than about most other breeds.

INFLUENCE OF THE COLLIE

The early settlers, who took sheep and cattle with them to Australia, naturally took dogs from the British Isles to work the stock. But conditions under which dogs work in the wildest parts of Scotland, Wales or the North of England, are mild by comparison with conditions which prevail 'down under'. The terrible heat and dusty, arid conditions found in many parts of Australia require far more stamina in both man and dog than the wind, rain, snow and blizzards of the UK – not that the Aussies don't have wind and rain, even snow too! There was, however, one species of dog which had lived and hunted with the Aborigine people under these conditions for thousands of years before the white man arrived. This was the Dingo, which might provide some hybrid vigour, if crossed with the imported working breeds. It is recorded that in about 1840 Thomas S. Hall, whose family owned around a quarter of a million acres of cattle grazing land in the Hunter valley, crossed a Dingo with two imported "Blue Merle Highland Collies" of proved working ability. Not surprisingly, the resulting pups were either blue or red, and much tougher than their Collie ancestry. They were also excellent workers.

It appears that the Halls developed a strain of Cattle Dog, which became known as Hall's Heelers, Queensland Heelers, Blue Heelers or Red Heelers. In its native country, the breed is still known by the latter three names. Blue merle was an unpopular colour with hill shepherds as it was difficult to see in the distance, and impossible against certain backgrounds. It is interesting to note that Kaleski considered the blue speckle an advantage in Cattle Dogs, as it made them difficult for the cattle to see. Working dogs always have been, and still are, bred for different jobs, as a result of which different strains have developed. A man wanting a dog to win sheep dog trials would be unlikely, and very unwise, to buy a pup from a drover's strain. It might look very similar to a trial-bred pup, but it would work very differently. Likewise, a strong-eyed dog would rarely be of much use to a drover. Some strains of working dogs do breed true to type, as a result of a very simple process of selective breeding. If a shepherd had a particularly good working dog, it is pretty certain that another shepherd would want a bitch mated to that dog. The unwritten rule was that the stud dog owner had pick of the dog pups, and, not surprisingly, he often picked the one that most resembled his own dog. Likewise, the bitch's owner might well pick the bitch pup most like the dam. That is why some shepherds always kept dogs, while others preferred bitches. A shepherd who worked for my father had the same strain of dogs in an unbroken line for over forty years, but he never bred any himself.

There were those who had a preference for a certain colour or certain markings. On a farm called Bertha, near Perth in Scotland, there was a well-known strain of blue dogs, and John often saw them driving cattle to Perth market. They were known as 'Bertha Blues' and nearly all the blue dogs in that area were from this strain. There were, of course, other strains of blue dogs, and our theory, for what it is worth, is that the blue merle Collies imported by Thomas Hall were from a strain of blues, as opposed to the odd one that cropped up in a litter. They were also likely to be from a droving strain, which were much tougher and rougher in their style of working, than the shepherd's dogs. John used to see stumpy tails among drovers' dogs quite commonly, and this could account for the Stumpy Tailed Cattle Dog.

We make no pretence to be geneticists, so these are only the views of laymen. However, there is no doubt that the Collies which were used as the foundation for the ACD, bore little resemblance to either the Rough or Smooth Collie seen in the show ring today. We have never seen or heard of a 'Smooth Highland Collie', but *Hutchinson's Dog Encyclopaedia* claims that the Bearded Collie was also known as the Highland Collie or Border Collie! For good measure, it adds that this was the breed referred to by James Hogg, the Ettrick Shepherd. That was written as recently as 1933/4, and it shows how little attention should be paid to breed descriptions. It is safe to assume that one half of the ACD was founded on blue merle *working* Collies, probably from Scotland, but possibly from Wales, where quite a lot of blue merles can still be found working.

THE GERMAN COOLIE

It does not seem to have occurred to anyone that the ACD could carry the blood of the German

The Dingo was described as being "More dog than wolf".

The Dingo is a handsome, strongly-built animal.

F. Prenzel.

Coolie. This type can be found today working in Australia, and is highly praised by those who own them. No one seems quite sure of its origin, or when it was introduced to Australia. Kaleski does not mention the breed, although it would appear to have been around in his day. It may not have been used in the evolution of the ACD, but it is smooth-haired, prick-eared, and comes in both blue and red merles, making it a possibility, if not a probability.

THE DINGO

On the other side, we have the Dingo, and more is known about the origins of this dog than of the Collie. When the first settlers arrived in Australia, they found dogs living around the native settlements. These were all of one breed, the Dingo or 'Warrigal', as the Aborigines called it. There is some difference of opinion as to how long this native dog had been in Australia, and some scientists claim that it has been there for ten thousand years. Fossilised remains, both human and canine, suggest that the Dingo has lived and hunted with the Aborigines for well over three thousand years.

What matters most to us is not how long the Dingo has been in existence, but what sort of animal it was and is. In his book *The Present State of Australia* (1830) Robert Dawson wrote:

"The wild dog, which is a kind of small wolf, is the largest carnivorous animal known in Australia. They are, however, more of the dog than the wolf, as has been proved by the breed becoming intermixed, in some instances with European dogs... The only mischief this animal has been accused of is that of taking young lambs and biting sheep, as dogs have been known to do in England... These animals subsist in the woods almost entirely upon kangaroos, and hunt them by scent, as an English spaniel would a hare. They never bark in hunting, or, indeed, upon any other occasion: and if we may judge from their very lean and mangy appearance, they either procure a very slender subsistence, or are much subject to disease... the natives are exceedingly attached to dogs of any kind: I never saw a tribe without some of them.

"The natives frequently take the wild dogs when they are puppies and domesticate them. They become in this way very much attached as the common European dog, but they never possess the same open countenance and manner, being shy and sneaking, and instead of barking at a stranger, they will lower their tails, creep up behind their masters, and look between his legs. Neither will they fight when attacked by other dogs, otherwise than throwing themselves on the ground and snapping at their opponents...The native dogs are of various colours, red, black, red-and-white, black-and-white and fawn."

In Shaw's *The Illustrated Book of Dogs*, published in 1881, W. K. Taunton wrote:

"The Dingo, or as it is called by the natives, 'Warrigal', is the wild dog of Australia, in which country it causes great annoyance and loss to the inhabitants by the havoc it makes among their flocks. Large numbers (of Dingoes) are annually being destroyed, so that in some parts of the country they are now becoming scarce. The colour is almost invariably a reddish-fawn, white feet and white tip to the tail are looked upon as typical of the breed.

"The Dingo stands about 22 inches at the shoulder, and is a strongly made, very active dog, with powerful jaws, and teeth unusually large in proportion to the size of the dog. I see no reason why the Dingo should not become domesticated as any other dog, within a short space of time. Possibly it might take a generation or two before their innate wildness would be bred out, but much would depend under what conditions the puppies were reared. There is a general impression that these dogs are treacherous, and not to be trusted. I have owned two of the breed and cannot say, as far as my experience goes, that I have found them so. My best specimen I gave to a friend in Paris, and I believe the dog is now located in the Jardin des Plantes."

A few years later in *Amongst the Aborigines* (1889), Carl Lumholtz tells of his efforts to find a Dingo to take with him on his next expedition, and he wrote:

"This was a very difficult matter, for Dingoes are so much more rare here (Queensland being shot out by Europeans) than further South in Australia, where natives can be seen followed by ten or twelve dogs, which are different breeds, for the Dingoes of the natives quickly mix with the shepherd dogs, greyhounds and terriers of the colonists. On the Herbert river there are rarely more than one or two Dingoes in each tribe, and as a rule they are of pure blood. The natives find them as puppies in the hollow trunks of trees, and rear them with greater care than they bestow on their own children... Its master never strikes but merely threatens it. He caresses it like a child, eats the fleas off it, and then kisses it on the snout.

"Though the Dingo is treated so well, it often runs away, especially in the pairing season, and at such times it never returns. Thus it never becomes perfectly domesticated; still it is very useful to natives for it has a keen scent and traces every kind of game; it never barks, and hunts less wildly than our own dogs, but very rapidly, frequently capturing game on the run. The Dingo will follow nobody else but its owner; this naturally increased difficulty in finding a dog, for it was useless, unless the owner could be persuaded to go with me."

One of the most interesting and somewhat surprising pieces of information we have found in our research on the Dingo is in *The Twentieth Century Dog*, edited by Herbert Compton, and published in 1904. It is in two volumes, and the Dingo is included under 'Foreign Sporting Dogs'. Herbert Compton wrote:

"My illustration represents Myall, a red coloured dog, weighing 50lbs and standing 21 inches at shoulder, winner of 50 prizes, and the property of Mr H. C. Brooke, who writes of him as follows:-

" 'The Dingo is in colour and shape the handsomest of all breeds; his intelligence is very great, and what I am very fond of is his independent nature. He never takes to strangers, and there is no slavishness or cringing about him. He is his master's pal, but his master is only his owner – not his boss. The cunning and intelligence of the Dingo is well known to Australians, a pair of Dingoes have, on occasion, been known to pass through a flock of unshorn sheep, leaving them untouched, to reach a flock of shorn ones in an inner fold, which they could more easily worry.

" 'The first time old Myall was ever shown, soon after he arrived from Australia, was at Crufts some years ago. He got a nasty bite through the forefoot from an Elkhound in the ring. This was attended to by Mr Cawdle, and each morning, when Mr Cawdle approached the kennel he was in, this wild dog put his paw out for him to examine. At that time I was three miles from the nearest station, and as Myall refused to walk (on account of his paw), I ordered a cab to meet me at the station. However, it failed to turn up, and no other vehicle being available, I started to walk, carrying Myall on my shoulder, and leading a Bulldog. After about two miles on the road Myall spied a sheep stuck in the hedge, and jumped down and made for it. After that he evidently realised that it was no good shamming to be lame, and went on all right. Only I wished the sheep had occurred earlier in the walk!

" 'Myall was an excellent worker with ferrets. His son Chelsworth Myall, will also work with ferrets, and is a grand watchdog and personal protector. He is, however, sometimes uncomfortably ferocious, his mother, Macquarie Belle, having been an absolutely untamable bitch, and when he has a bad tempered fit on, he will go for anything, no matter what it is.' "

THE DINGO-CROSS

Dingoes, it would appear, created very different impressions on different people. It is clear, however, that it was well-known at the turn of the century that the Dingo could easily be domesticated. It was, therefore, quite natural that the early cattlemen would use the breed to improve the ability of their own dogs to work, and keep on working, under Australian conditions. Kaleski claims that the object was to produce a dog that worked silently, but many Collies never bark when working, and neither do a lot of Kelpies. Kaleski is adamant that there is no Dingo in the Kelpie, but there are others who disagree. It is certainly a less unlikely possibility than Kaleski's theory that the Kelpie was produced from a fox-dog cross!

So far as the ACD is concerned, there seems to be no doubt that the Dingo plays a big part in its evolution, much bigger, we suspect, than many people realise. Since we became interested in the breed, several Australians have told us of working Heelers, which have more than a dash of the native dog in them. Just before we started writing this book, we were at a dog show where we met an Australian on a visit to England. He told us of an exceptionally good working dog that he knew, which was one-quarter Dingo.

In 1903 Robert Kaleski wrote:

"Finding the strain is beginning to run out a little in shape and head, we are now crossing with a pet Dingo of mine to get these points back again, and although we will get a little too much red at first, I think the increased vigour and shape will more than repay me. I have a good deal of experience with the Dingo cross, and find it all right if sufficient care is exercised in the selection."

This last remark is most important. From what has been written about the breed, it is obvious that temperament varies enormously. An article appeared in the *Ipswich Times* and told how three Dingo pups were taken from a nest in the Woolgoola Ranges by Aboriginals. They were reared in the tribal camp and the most friendly of the three was eventually sent to Mr Kaleski in Sydney. It was quite legal to keep a Dingo in those days, a state of affairs which was to change dramatically.

PERSECUTION OF THE DINGO

As the European settlers extended their territories, they killed off as many of the native grazing animals as possible – and not a few of the native people – so that they would have more grass for their imported domestic animals. Deprived of kangaroos and wallabies as its main source of food, the Dingo was forced to look elsewhere. And there it was – mutton on a plate, so to speak.

As sheep became more numerous, so the calls for war against the Dingo, 'indiscriminate killer of sheep', became louder. A wild dog destruction board was set up, and the Dingo was declared a noxious animal with a bounty on its head. No one was allowed to keep one without a special licence – usually only granted to zoos – and it was an offence not to report anyone breaking this law. A Dingo fence was built in stages to divide the sheep country from the cattle country, where the wild dog is not such a menace. Reaching from the coast of South Australia to the Southern Queensland coast, this fence stretches for 3,750 miles (6,000km) – the longest fence in the world (the Great Wall of China is 1,684 miles long). But Dingoes still managed to get through, and the fence had to be maintained by a huge army of 'doggers'.

They shot, trapped and poisoned thousands upon thousands of the native dogs, without eradicating them. Modern technology was used to drop bait, laced with strychnine or 1080 poison from planes. This killed off a lot of Dingoes, as well as domestic cats and dogs, birds of prey, and anything else that would eat meat. However, the native dog is still around and is likely to be for some time to come. Doggers are paid according to the number of scalps they hand in, and it is unlikely that they will try too hard to exterminate their own source of livelihood!

CHANGING ATTITUDES

To call an Australian 'a Dingo', was, at the time, akin to calling an Englishman 'a rat'. But in spite

Berenice Walters of Wooleston ACD fame, and founder of the Australian Native Dog Training Society at Bargo, NSW, pictured with Dingoes.

New Idea.

of this, there are many quotes from doggers – who have spent most of their lives killing these animals – praising the courage, tenacity and extreme intelligence of the Dingo. Even in Australia, where some people still believe that the only good Dingo is a dead one, attitudes have changed in recent times. Considerable research has been carried out by the the Commonwealth Scientific & Industrial Research Organisation (CSIRO), which shows that the diet of the Dingo consists mainly of rabbits, lizards, rodents, wallabies and kangaroos. It varies according to the season, especially during droughts, but some experiments show as little as four per cent freshly killed sheep in the diet. It has also been found that where the Dingo population has been dramatically reduced, so the population of rabbits, wild pigs and kangaroos has increased, sometimes to plague proportions. Some say the financial losses caused by these pests are greater than the losses caused by Dingoes, but, of course, that might change if all controls were removed.

The fact that it was a serious offence to keep a tame Dingo does not mean that it was never done. It is not what you do that gets you into trouble; being found out is what matters! In the early seventies several people in Australia kept tame Dingoes, which they referred to as 'dogs'. They even took them to training classes, and there was one at a class where we were instructing during our visit in 1979.

One of the Dingo owners at this time was Berenice Walters, owner of the famous Wooleston strain of Australian Cattle Dogs. With the help of a few enthusiasts, she founded the Australian Native Dog Training Society of New South Wales, in 1976. Headquarters were at the Wooleston kennels at Bargo, NSW, where Berenice has now established a breeding unit for Dingoes. This has been given official approval, and a Breed Standard has been drawn up. Members of the Society have taken their native dogs on public parades, and to schools and other public places. Interested parties can visit the kennels. All of this is greatly increasing the public's understanding of this

'Snowgoose', trained to jump on command, pictured at the Merigal Dingo Education Centre.

B. Walters.

much maligned and misunderstood animal. On our second visit to Australia in 1984, we visited Wooleston, which we found very interesting and sometimes surprising. Type and coat vary considerably, from thick, double-coated, bushy-tailed types from the Snowy Mountains, to the smooth, single-coated inhabitants of the tropical areas of the North. In between is the type most often seen in zoos, with a short, dense double-coat. Colour also varies from pure white to pure black, while white socks and a white tip to the tail are quite common. The most common colour is red or fawn of varying shades.

As a result of more people taking an interest in the Dingo, there is a much greater knowledge of its character and temperament. Many years ago I was asked to train a Dingo. The lady had acquired the bitch as a pup from one of the zoos, but had been unable to train her, and hoped that I might succeed. But the bitch was so nervous that I had no success at all; she had not been socialised, but I doubt if she would have been trainable, even if she had been.

At Bargo, the Walters had a male Dingo, called Napoleon, who lived in the house like any other

The male Dingo, 'Snowdrift', pictured at Bargo, with two of his offspring. The male takes an active role in rearing the pups from the time they are about five weeks old. Note the black spot on the pup's tail, a feature on many ACDs, but not mentioned in the Breed Standard.

dog. He was a big, handsome, dark-coloured dog of the tropical type, and had qualified CD in Obedience Trials. Strangers he treated with aloof disdain, but he wasn't at all afraid of them and tolerated them touching him. To his own family, he was the complete opposite, being extremely affectionate and submissive. He always slept on the bed, and he never showed any sign of aggression. In short, Napoleon combined many of the desirable characteristics so often lacking in today's pedigree dogs.

We saw a lot of other Dingoes at Bargo. Some were very nervous and timid; most were very affectionate towards their owners, and some were quite friendly towards strangers. None were at all aggressive. It should be remembered that man has persecuted and harassed the Dingo for two centuries. Like the wolf, which has suffered the same fate for even longer, the bold, fearless Dingo is much more likely to become a dead Dingo than the timid, furtive type, which will live to transmit its genes to the next generation. However, some of the old doggers have tales of bold, arrogant Dingoes, which have used their intelligence to evade traps, poison and guns for years. The Australian Native Dog Training Society is proving that a lot of Dingoes can be domesticated and trained to become affectionate companions.

After all the years of survival against all the odds, there is now a very real risk that the wild Dingo could become extinct – not by man's almost fanatical efforts to exterminate it, but by man's own carelessness. So many domestic dogs have been allowed to 'go bush' and have mated with Dingoes, that it is estimated that in parts of Australia only ten per cent of the wild dog population is pure Dingo.

THE SMITHFIELD

Historians of the ACD mention several breeds other than the Collie. Several references are made to the Smithfield, a type local to East Anglia, UK, and used by drovers who took herds and flocks to London's Smithfield market. John knew a shepherd, a native of Suffolk, born at the beginning of this century, who told him that dogs known as Smithfields were a mixture of Old English Sheepdog and Collie. They had come down from Scotland when fairly large numbers of Scottish farmers had travelled south with their sheep, and settled in East Anglia. What is not known, is what influence, if any, these breeds had on the end product. If the introduction of new blood proves to be a success, the progeny are likely to be bred from, and so have a lasting influence on the breed. However, if it is not a success, the progeny are unlikely to be bred from, and the new blood will have no influence at all on the breed.

THE BULL TERRIER

There is evidence that Bull Terrier blood was used in the formation of the ACD. This is quite likely, as the breed was very popular with early settlers in all former British colonies, and was often, and still is, used to increase 'guts' in working breeds. The ACD bears some resemblance, both mentally and physically, to the Bull Terrier, with one important difference. The characteristic of the ACD is to grip and let go, while the Bull Terrier would tend to hang on, and for this reason it is doubtful whether it would have been used to any great extent.

THE DALMATIAN

A cross of Dalmatian was also used to give the breed a 'love of horses'! It is usually assumed that because the Dalmatian would run under a carriage, it was fond of horses. However, in the days when horses were the chief mode of transport, dogs of all breeds could be seen running under carts. We have had several dogs, including an ACD, who would run under a trap with virtually no training at all. What influence, if any, the Dalmatian would have had in the evolution of the ACD is hard to say; but some claim that it is the reason why the pups are born white, and also why deafness crops up from time to time.

THE KELPIE

There are differences of opinion as to whether Kelpie blood was used. As the ACD was established as a breed before the advent of the Kelpie, it is unlikely. But the Kelpie, like the ACD, is a direct descendant of working Collies from Scotland, and if extended pedigrees could be produced, we would not be surprised if the same names appeared in both breeds. Unfortunately, pedigrees in those days were kept in the minds of the breeders, and we have been unable to find any that were recorded. Even that prolific writer Robert Kaleski does not seem to have put any pedigrees on paper.

THE HEELER

The very early Heeler resembled 'a small thick-set Dingo', and this is highly likely, as the type of a very old, pure breed is nearly always dominant to that of a 'mixed up' breed. A Greyhound crossed with almost any other breed produces a Lurcher, which invariably has more resemblance to the Greyhound than to the other parent. Likewise, a part-bred Arab horse always has an 'Arab' look about it. However, it is surprising that, very early on, the ACD seems to have had no white markings, except a faint white mark on the forehead. A great majority of Collie and Sheepdog types have white legs, a white tip to the tail, and frequently a white ruff, while many Dingoes have white feet and a white tip to the tail. The fact that neither the ACD nor the Kelpie have any white could be due to the Australians trying to breed for dark pads. Many people, ourselves included, believe that dark pads do not blister so easily as light ones on hard going. Then along comes the Dingo, with white feet, to prove that there are no hard and fast rules in the animal world!

THE FIRST STANDARD

The early breeders appear to have been keen on type. Kaleski actually drew up his first Breed Standard in 1897, and revised it in 1903. This was at a time when owners of working dogs in UK were only interested in what the dog could do, irrespective of what it looked like. In spite of this, Collies were seen at dog shows, and when Queen Victoria purchased a Rough Collie in 1860, the breed became very popular, and by the turn of the century it was one of the most numerous at dog shows. At this time, John' s father, who was a horse dealer as well as a farmer, told him how he would buy a good-looking Collie if he happened to see one on a farm, but he never sold it to work. He could get far more for it from a breeder or dealer (who would sell it on to a breeder, perhaps in America) for far more than any farmer or shepherd would dream of paying. This is how some breeds became divided into working and show strains. Usually the gap between the two quickly becomes wider, ending up with two completely different types.

   This does not seem to have happened with the ACD. It is safe to assume that by the time Kaleski drew up his first Standard in 1897, there were considerable numbers of dogs around which were fairly uniform in type; this would be made easier by the fact that the Dingo type would appear dominant. By then, it was thirty-seven years since the first reported mating of a Dingo with a Collie. It is important to remember that the type which had evolved was the result of breeding from dogs that could do a particular job of work, as opposed to dogs which conformed to a standard of points. It is fortunate that the man who drew up the first Standard actually worked dogs. In *Barkers and Bit*ers he wrote:

   "In 1893, when I got rid of my cross-bred Cattle Dogs and took up the Blues, breeders of the latter had started breeding for certain colours and markings so as to ensure purity and fix the type." Later he wrote: "There have been several attempts to make pure breeds of Cattle dogs, but the only survivors are the Red and Blue Speckles. The others soon died out."

   Very few breeders are named in the literature we have read on the breed. Amongst them are the brothers, Jack and Harry Baghurst, who said that they "bred a lot and drowned a lot", which suggests that the pups didn't all come up to expectations. But it is unlikely that many stockmen would discard a mismarked pup that had potential working ability. Even today, there are a lot of very odd-looking Heelers working in Australia, and the odd mismarked or drop-eared pup crops up in strains bred for type for several generations. We have seen a litter which all had white markings on them, one of them predominantly white, and another was chocolate-coloured like a Kelpie.

Chapter Two

THE BREED STANDARD

CHARACTER AND TEMPERAMENT

Interesting as the history of a breed is, what really matters to us is what the breed is now; what has evolved from all that cross breeding, and no doubt some very close in-breeding. If you picked out ten breed books on ten different breeds, you would find that in every case the breed was good with children, easy to train, very intelligent and so on. There are two reasons for this. Firstly, the writers have never owned any other breed – some have never owned a dog at all! Secondly, many authors are breeders who regard themselves as ambassadors for the breed and feel they must, on no account, say anything detrimental about it. The fear of what rival breeders might say, if they attempted to be controversial, has something to do with this.

We believe that an author's responsibility is to the readers. Most people believe what they read in books – some even believe what they read in newspapers! But if someone is persuaded, by the exaggerated claims in a book, to buy a dog which is quite unsuited to their purpose, then that person is going to be bitterly disappointed, and the dog will be very unhappy. Far from doing the reputation of the breed any good, such claims can do it a lot of harm.

The great mistake made by most dog writers is to generalise. One of the worst offenders is Robert Kaleski, whom I have quoted so often. In all his references to various breeds and crosses, it is always "*they* do this" or "*they* do that." There is no such thing as a breed of dog – even less so a cross-breed – where all specimens will behave in the same way. Two puppies from the same litter, reared under identical conditions, will grow into two entirely different animals.

In no breed that we know is there a wider range of varying temperaments than in the ACD. This is not surprising when you consider the variation in the Dingo – an animal designed by nature, not by man. As previously quoted, Robert Dawson describes them (again generalising) as "being shy and sneaky – creep behind their masters and look between his legs." However, H. C. Brooke, describing his own Dingo, says that he "is a grand watchdog and personal protector. He is, however, sometimes uncomfortably ferocious – and when he has a bad-tempered fit on, he will go for anything, no matter what it is." Extremes as great as this are to be found in the present-day ACD. Even within the small population in the UK, I have seen temperaments ranging from the pathetically nervous to the dangerously aggressive.

Kaleski wrote: "Nothing in the bush makes as good a mate as a Cattle Dog. Besides working cattle and horses, he is a great fighter, good game dog, retriever and the finest watch dog possible." It is highly unlikely that every single Cattle Dog fitted this description, and Kaleski probably knew this perfectly well. However, it is safe to assume that the majority of the breed would answer that description. It would also be safe to assume that was the ideal, which most breeders of the day were aiming for. The ideal, that is, for a stockman living and working in the Australian outback. However, only a small minority of ACD owners have ever seen the Australian outback, and if they had, would be horrified at the idea of living there.

AGGRESSION

The early settlers, with considerable foresight and skill, crossed their imported working dogs with the native wild dog. By careful selective breeding they developed this into a breed superior to anything that had previously been seen – *for their purpose.* This very intelligent dog, excelling in courage, tenacity and agility is now expected to live quite happily in a breeding kennel, or as a family pet in suburbia, or even in a city. The large numbers which do adapt is nothing short of amazing; that some do not, is not really very surprising.

The very qualities which were regarded as assets by the early stockmen are often a liability today. "A great fighter", Kaleski said, in admiration. Fighting, we have always regarded as a confounded nuisance in a working dog, to say the least. We like a dog which concentrates on its work, and this is impossible if the dog is always looking round for some rival with whom to pick an argument. Most stockmen agree with that view. In Kaleski's day, ACDs were working in the sale yards in Sydney, where they were bound to meet dogs belonging to other drovers. Had they been as keen on fighting as Kaleski implies, I doubt if the breed would have become as popular as a cattle dog as it did.

Kaleski (and no doubt some of his fellow dog-fanciers) was something of a pugilist himself, and he actually had a chapter in support of dog fights in *Barkers and Biters.* Some macho owners admire a dog which "can look after himself", but with the ever-increasing anti-dog rules and regulations today, this can lead to serious trouble. The same applies to the breed's guarding instinct, a feature well recognised in its native country. Anyone who drives into an Australian farmstead, and sees a heeler running loose, will stay in his car – if he has any sense! Many of today's owners like to think that their dog will protect them if the occasion arose. But the over-protective dog can, and frequently does, lead to serious trouble, especially if it is not under complete control.

HUNTING INSTINCTS

Had we not owned ACDs before reading *Barkers and Biters*, I would not have believed the author's statement that "they do not want to go hunting at all." It seems incredible that the first cross with a wild dog would not want to hunt. I expect there are some that will contradict this, but we have never owned a true hunter, and many owners have told us how their dogs have a natural tendency to stay with them.

We have some ponies, sheep and cattle on rough grazing which abounds with rabbits and roe deer. Our ACDs will chase a rabbit or deer for a short distance only, and immediately come back. If John is busy mending a fence, he never needs to keep an eye on the dog; the dog is keeping an eye on him. The ACDs we have had will more or less ignore the sheep and ponies (they never completely ignore anything), but they will seize every opportunity to have a go at the cattle if they come anywhere near.

When we were in Australia, we were told that the old breeders, having decided on the pup they liked best, would pick it up out of the nest. They would then put it down on the ground and walk away. If the pup followed them, they kept it, if it did not follow, they shot it! This is, perhaps, a bit of 'Aussie' exaggeration, but we decided to try it out on a number of puppies as young as six weeks. And, yes, each one toddled after us, away from the rest of the litter: and, no, we didn't have to shoot any! We ran a family dog show at our place, and John once took an eight-week-old puppy out to see how it reacted. The pup was without a lead, and with no encouragement from John, the little dog followed him past all the other dogs and people. The pup would stop to talk to people, but then immediately look around to see where John had gone, and rush to catch up. There may be other breeds that would do this, but we do not know of one.

DRAWING UP A BREED STANDARD
Most Kennel Clubs publish Breed Standards for all the breeds which they recognise. Some Breed Standards have been in existence for a long time, and others have been drawn up quite recently. The object is to provide a blueprint of the ideal dog so that judges can judge "according to the Standard", as opposed to judging according to their own whims and fancies. However, it is not as simple as that.

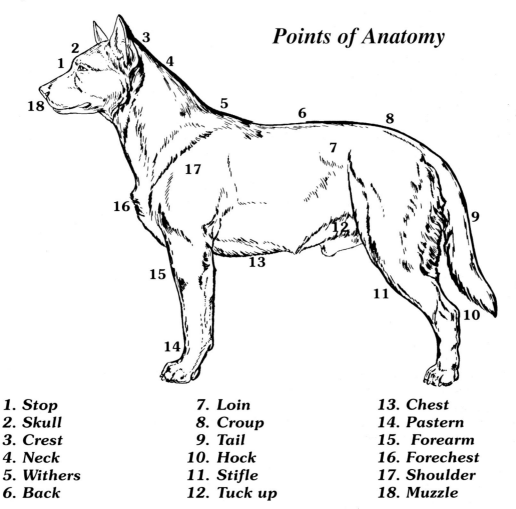

Points of Anatomy

1. Stop	*7. Loin*	*13. Chest*
2. Skull	*8. Croup*	*14. Pastern*
3. Crest	*9. Tail*	*15. Forearm*
4. Neck	*10. Hock*	*16. Forechest*
5. Withers	*11. Stifle*	*17. Shoulder*
6. Back	*12. Tuck up*	*18. Muzzle*

Like nearly all written descriptions, Standards are subject to different interpretations. How long is 'long', and how short is 'short'? Not to mention reasonably long, or fairly short! And that is not all. Different countries have different Standards for the same breed. The governing bodies of Australia, New Zealand, USA, Canada and the UK all publish different Standards for the ACD. That in spite of the fact that at the World Conference of Kennel Clubs in 1986 it was agreed by the controlling bodies that all Standards should be those of the country of origin.

The ACD must have been one of the first breeds to have its own Standard Of Points. This was drawn up by Robert Kaleski in 1897, and was recognised by the original Kennel Club of New South Wales in 1903. It was not changed until 1963.

STANDARD OF POINTS (1903)

DESCRIPTION	POINTS
Head: Broad between ears, tapering to a point at muzzle, full under the eye, strong and muscular in the jaws.	15
Ears: Short and pricked, running to a point at tip; thick, and set wide apart on the skull, with plenty of muscle at the butts. Should be as decidedly pricked as a cat's.	10
Eyes: Brown, quick, and sly-looking.	7
Shoulders: Strong, with good slope for free action.	7
Chest: Deep, but not out of proportion to body.	7
Legs: Clean, and fair amount of bone; great muscular development.	7
Feet: Small and cat-shaped.	7
Back: Straight, with ribs well sprung, ribbed up, and good loins; should arch slightly at loins.	7
Hindquarters: Strong and muscular, with back thighs well let down for speed; no dew-claws on feet; tail, fair length, Dingo or "bottle"-shaped.	12
Height: About 20 inches; bitches a little smaller.	7
Coat: Short, smooth and very dense.	7
Color: Head, black or red; body, dark blue on back (sometimes with black saddle) and black spot on tail-butt. Lighter blue, sometimes mottled with white hairs on underpart of body; legs, bluish, with red spots mottled over them. Tail, light blue, sometimes with white tip.	7
Total	**100**

General appearance: That of a small, thick-set blue Dingo.
Faults: Over- or under-size, legginess, half-prick or lopping ears, overshot or undershot jaws; anything likely to diminish speed and endurance.

KALESKI'S INTERPRETATION
Kaleski follows up his Standard of Points with a detailed analysis, which we quote from *Barkers and Biters*:

"We will now take the Standard point by point and explain it so that the judge and buyers can see the reason of each one.

Broad between ears: This ensures that the dog has a large brain-box, hence has plenty of intelligence. If narrow there, the brain must be small and the intelligence feeble; hence a poor worker.

Tapering to a point at muzzle: This means that the least weight is at the business end, ensuring that the dog can get his bite in quickly and drop out of danger, on the same principle as the boxer using light gloves instead of heavy ones – his hitting is much quicker.

Full under the eye: This ensures that the muscles which move the lower jaw are very strong, which is very necessary, as they correspond to the biceps of a boxer and give the dog power to do his work. A dog deficient there cannot continue biting long; his jaw-muscles become tired.

Strong and muscular in the jaws: If deficient there, when a dog is kicked by a shod horse he has his jaw broken because there is no cushion of muscle to protect the bone; hence, thus injured, he is useless.

Ears short and pricked: Short, so that they can be readily laid flat when biting or fighting; hence less likely to be damaged. Pricked, so as to catch sounds, such as whistles or words of command, best, especially from a distance. Running to a tip, V- or diamond-shaped, for two reasons: (1) the progeny are more likely to be prick-eared, the ear-muscles rising much higher in a diamond-ear than a "tulip" or spoon-shaped ear; (2) the spoon-ear is a sure indication of the Bull-terrier cross; set wide apart on the skull, so that the ear inclines outwards rather than forwards, for in the latter case they do not hear so well; hence cannot answer to the whistle or word of command as efficiently from a distance. They should be as pricked as a cat's for this reason.

Eyes, brown, because that is the Dingo color, therefore the best. If blue or white, the animal is extremely likely to go blind or deaf, or both; in either case it will be useless for anything.

Quick, because a dog has to judge his distance every time when coming in to bite, and the eye must be quick to do it.

Sly-looking, because a hot-headed, rushing dog is useless as a worker, and the eye is the index to his character.

Shoulders, strong and well-sloped, so that the dog gallops easily and drops with ease when biting.

Chest, deep, but not out of proportion to body: Deep, because a shallow-chested dog has no heartroom and is easily thrown off his balance. If too deep, or "Bulldoggy" as we call it, he cannot travel at any speed.

Legs: Clean, because a hairy-legged dog becomes weighted with mud on soft roads and soon tires. Fair amount of bone to carry a fairly heavy body. If too light in bone he is top-heavy. Great muscular development, because without it he lacks the driving power to do the work; hence he is useless.

Feet: Small and shaped like those of a cat, because offering the smallest bearing surface for heat-blisters on hot roads, or thorns ("bindyi"); also when the foot is small the power is more concentrated, giving better results. The shape of the foot was a disputed point for some years, some breeders arguing that the dog with the splay or "hare" foot sank less in soft ground, having a greater bearing surface. However, experience has proved that the cat foot is the best all round.

Back: Straight, because a hollow-backed dog is always weak in the loins, and hence cannot drop or come back quickly enough when biting.

Ribs: Well-sprung or "casky" denote a strong, hardy constitution; "well-ribbed up" means that the last rib is close to the hip, thus enabling the dog to turn and twist his body easily. Good loins, for the reason that they are the hinge of the body, and if weak the body is useless. Should arch slightly at loins, for the reason that the dog's hindquarters are then of the Greyhound shape, giving him more speed and activity than a straight-backed dog. If the reader looks at the prize-winners shown he will notice the slight arch in all of them. In my champion dog "Nugget", the arch is more pronounced; he was nearly as fast as a Greyhound, though very powerfully built.

Hindquarters: Strong and muscular, because they are the "engine" or propelling power of the dog. Some dogs are perfect in front, but fail lamentably here; such dogs tire very quickly, and do not earn their salt for a drover. Back thighs well let down for speed, because the lower the hock-joint the longer the stride; hence more speed. No dew-claws on feet, because they catch in long grass or mud and tear the sinew, crippling the dog.

Tail: Fair length, for the reason that it regulates the dog's movements, being merely a continuation of the backbone covered with hair, and it serves to balance the dog in his gallop. If too short or too long, his speed and action suffer accordingly, just as with Greyhounds. Dingo, or bottle-shape, for two reasons: (1) this shape of tail indicates Dingo strain, as against a long, thin tail denoting Bull-terrier, or a short tail the old Bob-tail; (2) a dog with a brush tail rests better than any other, as in a wild state the dog sleeps coiled in a circle, with the nose buried in the fur of the brush. I don't know why exactly, but believe that there is a physiological reason for it. Probably, by lessening the respiration in this way, the dog conserves energy on the same idea as hibernation – otherwise suspended animation.

Coat: Must be short, smooth and very dense, as the Cattle-dog has to work in all climates and all weathers. Like the Dingo, the coat consists of two – a loose outer one to turn the sun's rays, and a short inner one, close and fine as a seal's fur, to keep out cold and wet.

Height: About twenty inches has been found by experience to be the best height for working purposes. They work well in all heights, but do not stand the constant work like the dog of twenty inches; just as the medium-sized man is always the best for constant work, as against a big or a little one. Bitches, of course, should always be a little finer and smaller than the dog.

Color, for two reasons: (1) That true blue color (neither light nor dark) is the most invisible color possible, particularly at night; hence a dog of this color is not easily seen by cattle or horses, and thus has the least chance of being kicked. (2) The markings and colors as indicated stand for purity of breeding. In every strain of Blue Cattle-dog there is some peculiarity, and it shows in the color as well as in the shape, so that an expert can tell by looking at any Blue Dog how he has been bred. Some breeds have objectionable traits in their strains (Bull-terrier cross etc.), and the color helps as a guide to pedigree. If the dog shows more black than specified he is probably a Barb cross and hence timid and unreliable. If he is a whitey-blue he shows Dalmatian cross, and is very likely to be kicked or gored, especially at night, as stock can watch him much better; also he is more liable to go blind and deaf.

General appearance: That of a small, thick-set Dingo, for reasons given before.

Faults are specified so that the standard shall be rigidly adhered to and faults as described not allowed to creep in."

We find it difficult to follow Kaleski's points system, where, for instance, he awards more points for ears than for legs. But his description of the various points is brilliant and should be read by all judges of the breed. As the first Standard referred only to the "blues", there are those who believe that blue is the true colour of the breed. Before and after he drew up the Standard, Kaleski frequently refers to the blue and red speckles, and to the fact that they can be interbred without harm to either.

More surprising is the fact that the original Standard does not mention movement which we are sure, in those days, was considered more important than colour. Perhaps Kaleski simply assumed that no one was so stupid as to consider it unimportant! Nor does he refer to temperament, or that the dog should be amenable to handling in the show ring. Maybe the judges of the day regarded being bitten as an occupational hazard!

In 1963 the Australian National Kennel Council published a revised Standard, without the points chart. It added a clause on movement and on the red colour. It also said that "Whilst suspicious of strangers, must be amenable to handling, particularly in the show ring." Otherwise it was a condensed version of the original. Following the World Conference of Kennel Clubs in 1986, the ANKC revised the Standard with a view to bringing it into a format that would be agreeable to other countries.

ANKC BREED STANDARD (1987)

GENERAL APPEARANCE
The general appearance is that of a strong compact, symmetrically built working dog, with the ability and willingness to carry out his allotted task however arduous. Its combination of substance, power, balance and hard muscular condition must convey the impression of great agility, strength and endurance. Any tendency to grossness or weediness is a serious fault.

CHARACTERISTICS
As the name applies the dog's prime function, and one in which he has no peer, is the control and movement of cattle in both wide open and confined areas. Always alert, extremely intelligent, watchful, courageous and trustworthy, with an implicit devotion to duty making it an ideal dog.

TEMPERAMENT
The Cattle Dog's loyalty and protective instincts make it a self-appointed guardian to the Stockman, his herd and his property. Whilst naturally suspicious of strangers, must be amenable to handling, particularly in the Show ring. Any feature of temperament or structure foreign to a working dog must be regarded as a serious fault.

HEAD & SKULL
The head is strong and must be in balance with other proportions of the dog and in keeping with its general conformation. The broad skull is slightly curved between the ears, flattening to a slight but definite stop. The cheeks muscular, neither coarse nor prominent with the under jaw strong, deep and well developed. The foreface is broad and well filled in under the eyes, tapering gradually to form a medium length, deep, powerful muzzle with the skull and muzzle on parallel planes. The lips are tight and clean. Nose black.

EYES
The eyes should be of oval shape and medium size, neither prominent nor sunken and must express alertness and intelligence. A warning or suspicious glint is characteristic when approached by strangers. Eye colour, dark brown.

EARS
The ears should be of moderate size, preferably small rather than large, broad at the base, muscular, pricked and moderately pointed neither spoon nor bat eared. The ears are set wide apart on the skull, inclining outwards, sensitive in their use and pricked when alert, the leather should be thick in texture and the inside of the ear fairly well furnished with hair.

MOUTH
The teeth, sound, strong and evenly spaced, gripping with a scissor-bite, the lower incisors close behind and just touching the upper. As the dog is required to move difficult cattle by heeling or biting, teeth which are sound and strong are very important.

NECK

The neck is extremely strong, muscular, and of medium length broadening to blend into the body and free from throatiness.

FOREQUARTERS

The shoulders are strong, sloping, muscular and well angulated to the upper arm and should not be too closely set at the point of the withers. The forelegs have strong, round bone, extending to the feet and should be straight and parallel when viewed from the front, but the pasterns should show flexibility with a slight angle to the forearm when viewed from the side. Although the shoulders are muscular and the bone is strong, loaded shoulders and heavy fronts will hamper correct movement and limit working ability.

BODY

The length of the body from the point of the breast bone, in a straight line to the buttocks, is greater than the height at the withers, as 10 is to 9. The topline is level, back strong with ribs well sprung and carried well back not barrel ribbed. The chest is deep, muscular and moderately broad with the loins broad, strong and muscular and the flanks deep. The dog is strongly coupled.

HINDQUARTERS

The hindquarters are broad, strong and muscular. The croup is rather long and sloping, thighs long, broad and well developed, the stifles well turned and the hocks strong and well let down. When viewed from behind, the hind legs, from the hocks to the feet, are straight and placed parallel, neither close nor too wide apart.

FEET

The feet should be round and the toes short, strong, well arched and held close together. The pads are hard and deep, and the nails must be short and strong.

TAIL

The set on of tail is moderately low, following the contours of the sloping croup and of length to reach approximately to the hock. At rest it should hang in a very slight curve. During movement or excitement the tail may be raised, but under no circumstances should any part of the tail be carried past a vertical line drawn through the root. The tail should carry a good brush.

GAIT/MOVEMENT

The action is true, free, supple and tireless and the movement of the shoulders and forelegs is in unison with the powerful thrust of the hindquarters. The capability of quick and sudden movement is essential. Soundness is of paramount importance and stiltiness, loaded or slack shoulders, straight shoulder placement, weakness at elbows, pasterns or feet, straight stifles, cow or bow hocks, must be regarded as serious faults. When trotting the feet tend to come closer together at ground level as speed increases, but when the dog comes to rest he should stand four square.

COAT

The coat is smooth, a double coat with a short dense undercoat. The outercoat is close, each hair straight, hard, and lying flat, so that it is rain-resisting.

Under the body, to behind the legs, the coat is longer and forms near the thigh a mild form of breeching. On the head (including the inside of the ears), to the front of the legs and feet, the hair is short. Along the neck it is longer and thicker. A coat either too long or too short is a fault. As an average, the hairs on the body should be from 2.5 to 4cm (approx 1-1 1/2ins) in length.

COLOUR
Blue: The colour should be blue, blue-mottled or blue speckled with or without other markings. The permissible markings are black, blue or tan markings on the head, evenly distributed for preference. The forelegs tan midway up the legs and extending up the front to breast and throat, with tan on jaws; the hindquarters tan on inside of hindlegs, and inside of thighs, showing down the front of the stifles and broadening out to the outside of the hindlegs from hock to toes. Tan undercoat is permissible on the body providing it does not show through the blue outer coat. Black markings on the body are not desirable.
Red Speckle: The colour should be of good even red speckle all over, including the undercoat, (neither white or cream), with or without darker red markings on the head. Even head markings are desirable. Red markings on the body are permissible but not desirable.
SIZE: Height: The height at the withers should be Dogs 46 to 51 centimetres (approx. 18-20 inches). Bitches 43 to 48 centimetres (approx. 17-19 inches).
FAULTS
Any departure from the foregoing points should be considered a fault and the seriousness with which the fault should be regarded should be in exact proportion to its degree.
NOTE: Male animals should have two apparently normal testicles fully descended into the scrotum.
Approved by the ANKC, 1987. Reproduced by kind permission of the ANKC.

At the time of writing, the UK has no official Breed Standard. It only has an Interim Standard, which was drawn up without the co-operation, or even the knowledge, of the ACD Society of GB – the only society catering for the breed in the UK. The society has suggested a number of amendments, and it is hoped that these will be accepted by the Kennel Club.

BRITISH INTERIM STANDARD
GENERAL APPEARANCE Strong, compact, symmetrical, with substance, power and balance. Hard muscular condition conveys agility, strength and endurance. Grossness or weediness undesirable.
CHARACTERISTICS Ability to control and move cattle in all environments. Loyal, protective. Guardian of stockman, herd and property. Naturally suspicious of strangers, but amenable to handling. Biddable.
TEMPERAMENT Alert, intelligent, watchful, courageous, trustworthy, devoted to its work.
HEAD AND SKULL Strong, in balance with body and general conformation. Skull broad and slightly curved between ears, flattening to slight but definite stop. Cheeks muscular but not coarse or prominent. Strong under-jaw, deep and well developed. Broad foreface, well filled in under eyes, tapers gradually down medium length muzzle which is parallel to skull. Nose always black.
EYES Medium, oval, alert and intelligent, dark brown. Neither prominent nor sunken. Warning suspicious glint is characteristic.
EARS Moderate, small rather than large. Broad at base, muscular, pricked and moderately pointed. Oval or bat-eared undesirable. Set wide apart inclining outwards. Sensitive, pricked when alert. Leather thick in texture and inside ear well furnished with hair.
MOUTH Lips tight and clean. Jaws strong with a perfect, regular and complete scissor bite, i.e. the upper teeth closely overlapping the lower teeth and set square to the jaws.
NECK Exceptionally strong, muscular, of medium length blending into body. Free from throatiness.

FOREQUARTERS Strong, sloping shoulders well laid back, not too closely set at withers. Strong, round bone, legs straight when viewed from front, pasterns flexible and slightly sloping when viewed from side. Loaded shoulder and heavy front undesirable.

BODY Slightly longer from point of shoulder to buttocks than height at withers, as 10 is to 9. Level topline, strong back and couplings. Well sprung ribs, carried well back, but not barrel ribbed. Chest deep muscular and moderately broad.

HINDQUARTERS Broad, strong and muscular. Croup rather long and sloping. Well turned stifle, hocks strong and well let down. When viewed from behind, hocks to feet straight and set parallel, neither too close nor too wide apart.

FEET Round, short toes, strong, well arched and held tight, pads hard and deep. Nails short and strong.

TAIL Set on low, following slope of croup/rump. Reaching to back hanging in slight curve at rear. When working or excited, may be raised but never carried over back. Good brush.

GAIT/MOVEMENT True, free, supple, tireless, with powerful thrust of hindquarters. Capable of quick and sudden action. Soundness of paramount importance. Stands four square, but when moving at speed, legs tend to converge. Any weaknesses highly undesirable.

COAT Smooth, double with short dense undercoat. Close top coat hard, straight and weather resistant. Under body and behind legs, coat is longer to form mild breeching near thighs. Short on head (including inside of ear) front of legs and feet. Thicker and longer on neck. Average hair length 2.5 cm. (l-l1/2 in.).

COLOUR

BLUE Blue, blue-mottled or blue speckled with or without other markings. Permissible markings are black, blue or tan markings on head, evenly distributed for preference. Forelegs tan midway up legs and extending up the front to breast and throat, with tan on jaws. Hindquarters tan on inside of hindlegs, and inside of thighs, showing down front of stifles and broadening out to outside of hindlegs from hock to toes. Tan undercoat permissible on body providing it does not show through blue outer coat. Black markings on body undesirable.

RED SPECKLE Good even red speckle all over, including undercoat, (neither white nor cream), with or without darker red markings on head. Even head markings desirable. Red markings on body permissible but undesirable.

SIZE Height at withers: Dogs 46-51 cm. (approx. 18-20 in.); Bitches 43-48 cm. (17-19 in.).

FAULTS Any departure from the foregoing points should be considered a fault and the seriousness with which the fault should be regarded should be in exact proportion to its degree.

Note: Male animals should have two apparently normal testicles fully descended into the scrotum.

Reproduced by kind permission of the English Kennel Club.

The American Kennel Club published a Breed Standard in 1979 which is very similar to the Australian Standard.

AMERICAN BREED STANDARD

GENERAL APPEARANCE: The general appearance is that of a sturdy, compact, symmetrically-built working dog. With the ability and willingness to carry out any task however arduous, its combination of substance, power, balance and hard muscular condition to be such that must convey the impression of a great agility, strength and endurance. Any tendency to grossness or weediness is a serious fault.

CHARACTERISTICS:The utility purpose is assistance in the control of cattle, in both wide open and confined areas. Ever alert, extremely intelligent, watchful, courageous and trustworthy, with an implicit devotion to duty, making it an ideal dog. Its loyalty and protective instincts make it a self-appointed guardian to the stockman, his herd, his property. Whilst suspicious of strangers, must be amenable to handling in the show ring.

HEAD: The head, in balance with other proportions of the dog, and in keeping with its general conformation, is broad of skull. and only slightly curved between the ears, flattening to a slight but definite stop. The cheeks are muscular, but not coarse nor prominent, the underjaw is strong, deep and well-developed. The foreface is broad and well filled in under the eye, tapering gradually to a medium length, deep and powerful muzzle. The lips are tight and clean. The nose is black irrespective of the color of the dog.

Teeth – The teeth should be sound, strong. and regularly spaced, gripping with a scissors-like action, the lower incisors close behind and just touching the upper. Not to be undershot nor overshot.

Eyes – The eyes should be oval shaped of medium size, neither prominent nor sunken, and must express alertness and intelligence. A warning or suspicious glint is characteristic. Eye color is dark brown.

Ears – The ears should be of moderate size, preferably small rather than large, broad at the base, muscular, pricked and moderately pointed (not spoon nor bat eared). Set wide apart on the skull, inclined outwards, sensitive in their use, and only erect when alert. The inside of the ear should be fairly well furnished with hair.

NECK: The neck is of exceptional strength, muscular, and of medium length broadening to blend into the body and free from throatiness.

FOREQUARTERS: The shoulders are broad of blade, sloping, muscular and well angulated to the upper arm, and at the point of the withers should not be too closely set. The forelegs have strong round bone, extending to the feet without weakness at the pasterns. The forelegs should be perfectly straight viewed from the front, but the pasterns should show a slight angle with the forearm when regarded from the side.

HINDQUARTERS: The hindquarters are broad, strong and muscular. The rump is rather long and sloping, thighs long, broad and well-developed, with moderate turn to stifle. The hocks are strong and well let down. When viewed from behind, the hind legs, from the hocks to the feet, are straight and placed neither close nor too wide apart.

FEET: The feet should be round and the toes short, strong, well-arched and held together. The pads hard and deep, and the nails must be short and strong.

BODY: The length of the body from the point of the breast bone, in a straight line to the buttocks, is greater than the height at the withers, as 10 is to 9. The topline is level, back strong, with ribs well sprung and ribbed back. (Not barrel ribbed.) The chest is deep and muscular, and moderately broad, loins are broad. deep and muscular with deep flanks strongly coupled between the fore and hindquarters.

TAIL: The set on of the tail is low, following the contours of the sloping rump, and at rest should hang in a slight curve of a length to reach approximately to the hock. During movement and/or excitement it may be raised, but under no circumstances should any part of the tail be carried past a vertical line drawn through the root.

COAT: The weather resisting outer coat is moderately short, straight and of medium texture, with short dense undercoat. Behind the quarters the coat is longer, forming a mild breeching. The tail is furnished sufficiently to form a good brush. The head, forelegs, hind legs from hock to ground, are coated with short hair.

COLOR (Blue): The color should be blue or blue-mottled with or without other markings. The permissible markings are black, blue or tan markings on the head, evenly distributed for preference. The forelegs tan midway up the legs and extending up the front to the breast and throat, with tan on jaws; the hindquarters tan on inside of hind legs, and inside of thighs, showing down from the front of the stifles and broadening out to the outside of the hind legs from hock to toes. Tan undercoat is permissible on the body providing it does not show through the blue outer coat. Black markings on the body are not desirable.

COLOR (Red Speckle): The color should be a good even red speckle all over including the undercoat (not white or cream) with or without darker red markings on the head. Even head markings are desirable. Red markings on the body are permissible but not desirable.

SIZE: The desirable height at the withers to be within the following dimensions:—
Dogs 18 to 20 inches.
Bitches 17 to 19 inches.
Dogs or bitches over or under these specified sizes are undesirable.

MOVEMENT: Soundness is of paramount importance. The action is true, free, supple and tireless, the movement of the shoulders and forelegs with the powerful thrust of the hindquarters, in unison. Capability of quick and sudden movement is essential. Stiltiness, loaded or slack shoulders. straight shoulder placement, weakness at elbows, pasterns or feet, straight stifles, cow or bow hocks, must be regarded as serious faults.

Approved June 12, 1979. Reproduced by kind permission of The American Kennel Club.

INTERPRETATION BASED ON THE ANKC (COUNTRY OF ORIGIN) STANDARD

Canada and New Zealand also have their own Breed Standards, while South Africa, Kenya and some European countries use the British Standard. The Canadian Standard disqualifies dogs with yellow eyes, with undershot or overshot mouths, and those measuring under or over half an inch outside the standard height. With the exception of the English and Canadian Standards, there is little fundamental difference between any of the others. In studying them all, we get the impression that the governing bodies employ people who amuse themselves by altering the wording and layout of a text, without altering the meaning! That the "good brush" comes under the 'Tail' heading in one, and under 'Coat' in another, is only one of many examples.

There is one big weakness in all Standards relating to Working Breeds. For most of our lives, we have mixed with people who work dogs, but we have never known anyone who claimed to be able to tell whether or not a dog would work by simply looking at it. Even if it is known that it will work, it is still quite impossible to say *how* it will do so. "Any feature of temperament foreign to a working dog," states the Standard "must be regarded as a serious fault." But what temperament is foreign to a working dog? Few nervous dogs will face cattle, but some do. They may bolt for home if someone shouts at them, and they may let you down just when they are most needed. But providing the instinct to work is stronger than the dog's natural fear, that dog will work, sometimes very well, under normal circumstances.

Likewise an over-aggressive dog, anxious to take on not only all the other dogs in the ring, but the judge as well, can be an excellent cattle dog. This may or may not be too aggressive towards cattle, but the only way to find out is to see the dog work. Obviously, dogs cannot be seen working in the show ring, so all the judge can do is to assume that the dog will work (the vast majority will), and decide whether or not the dog is *structurally capable of doing so.* It is unfortunate that very few judges have ever seen a dog working cattle, and some have never seen a dog do any sort of work. All the judge has to go by is the Standard of Points, or, more accurately, his interpretation of it. Most of the Standard is fairly straightforward, so we shall only deal with those parts which we feel can cause confusion.

TEMPERAMENT

"Whilst naturally suspicious of strangers, must be amenable to handling, particularly in the show ring." This is very different from, and much more important than, referring to any feature of temperament "foreign to a working dog." It is sometimes very difficult to decide whether a dog is suspicious of strangers or afraid of them, on meeting the dog for the first time. If a dog curls up its lip or growls at a judge, some owners will say, "But the breed is *supposed* to be suspicious of strangers."

On the other hand, we have had several dogs who were suspicious of strangers to the point of disliking them. When running free they would simply avoid the outstretched hand, which wanted to touch them, and people would say, "What a pity he's so nervous." But he wasn't nervous, nor was he afraid of strangers, he just didn't like them, and there were occasions when we didn't blame him! On a lead the same dog would be handled by anyone without protest. There were two reasons for this. Firstly, the dog could not get away from the stranger. Secondly, a dog in close proximity to a respected pack leader (in this case, the handler) should react to the stranger in the same way as the pack leader reacts.

The British Interim Standard leaves out "particularly in the show ring", and we have heard it argued that this is better. The reason given is that the dog should be amenable to handling at any time, but this does not stipulate by whom the dog has to be handled; whereas by referring to the show ring, it means that the dog has to be handled by the judge, who is likely to be a complete stranger. In any case, Breed Standards are intended to guide judges in the show ring.

Before leaving the subject of temperament, it is worth noting that only a minority of ACDs ever see a cow, let alone have the opportunity to work, even in their native country. The vast majority of puppies end up as companions and guards. A stable temperament is, therefore, absolutely essential. While it is impossible to tell by looking at a dog whether or not that dog will work, it is possible to form a fairly accurate impression of temperament. Handling a dog can help in this direction, although it has to be admitted that some judges seem experts at frightening shy puppies, and bringing out the aggression in aggressive dogs. Our observations suggest that judges in the USA pay far more attention to temperament than those in the UK or Australia. In some European countries all dogs have to pass a strict temperament test before they can be used for breeding or can become Champions.

HEAD

"The head is strong and must be in balance with other proportions of the dog." In other words, it must not be too strong, nor should it be snipey or weak in any way. The Standard does not say that a male should be masculine and a female feminine. Strangely enough, very few Breed Standards highlight this point, but it is not uncommon for judges' critiques to refer to a dog as being too effeminate, although bitches are rarely described as being too masculine.

Over the years, we have found that 'doggy' bitches are frequently excellent workers, but we have never known a 'bitchy' dog that was worth the food he ate. On the other hand, the best breeding bitches are usually the ones with a certain female 'quality' about them. In any case, we

Heads in profile (Formakin Kulta, and his dam, Aust. Ch. Landmaster Darling Red) showing "slight but definite stop."

R. Willbie.

think it is very important to be able to tell whether an animal is male or female when meeting it head on.

EYES
The "warning or suspicious glint in the eye when approached by strangers" is difficult to define. It is very typical of the breed, but it does not mean that the dog is about to bite; neither does it mean that it won't bite – which may well be why the Australians inserted the "amenability to handling" clause!

Temperament is usually reflected in the eyes which may show suspicion of a stranger, but should never show fear. They should be bright, alert and express intelligence, although it is impossible to assess the degree of intelligence by simply looking at a dog.

Obviously the eyes must not be prominent in a dog which frequently has to work under extremely dusty conditions. The colour should be dark brown. Many people believe that a light eye is a sign of unreliable temperament, but we have known some very nice dogs with light eyes – and also some very nasty ones with dark eyes. Wolves have light eyes which may have given rise to the prejudice against them. However, John has handled tame wolves with much steadier temperaments than some of the dark-eyed dogs he has handled. The Standard calls for a dark-brown eye, and that is the colour most people like. Obviously, wall eyes which crop up occasionally in the blues, are quite wrong. Incidentally, Dingoes have dark eyes.

EARS
These are fairly well described in the Standard. In many cases, ears are too big and the leather is too thin. Sometimes they drop forward, fold out sideways or just fly about. The ears should be strong like a Dingo's. The Standard states that they should "be sensitive in their use and pricked

The ACD should look typically masculine (Formakin Kulta, left) or feminine (Formakin Brolga, right). Both dogs have ears set wide apart on the skull, and they are placed at the correct angle. Kulta (left) has superior ears in that they are slightly smaller in proportion to the head, and they are also thicker, and therefore more muscular.

R. Willbie.

when alert." We have yet to see a judge of ACDs paying any attention to how the dog uses its ears, while all handlers seem to concentrate on getting the dog to keep its ears pricked all the time. When a dog is stacked, with the lead held tight up behind its ears, it cannot use them. This, we think, is a pity as a lot can be learned about a dog's character by the way it uses its ears.

MOUTH
The teeth should meet with a scissor bite, the lower incisors close behind and just touching the upper. Although the Standard says that teeth should be strong, as they will be used for biting cattle, it only refers to incisors. It is the canines which are used for biting, and the premolars and molars for eating. Missing molars seem to be more common than they used to be in many breeds, including the ACD. Some judges only look at the front of a dog's mouth, but an increasing number are now examining the side to see if any molars or premolars are missing. In some countries this is considered a much more serious fault than in others. It is unlikely that a dog misses one or even two teeth any more than we do, but if allowed to creep in, hereditary defects like this can quickly become worse

THE OVERALL STRUCTURE
The neck, forequarters, body and hindquarters are all well described, but it is important to consider them altogether, and not divide them up into 'joints'. The whole should be balanced, and all parts in proportion to each other. We should consider why the Standard calls for them to be as stipulated. Just as a Greyhound has to be able to bend down and pick up a hare, so a Cattle Dog must be able to bend down, turn its head sideways, and bite the heel of a cow. Both breeds must achieve this without slowing down, which is why both require strong necks of fair length, nicely moulded into the shoulder. The shoulders should not be too close together at the withers.

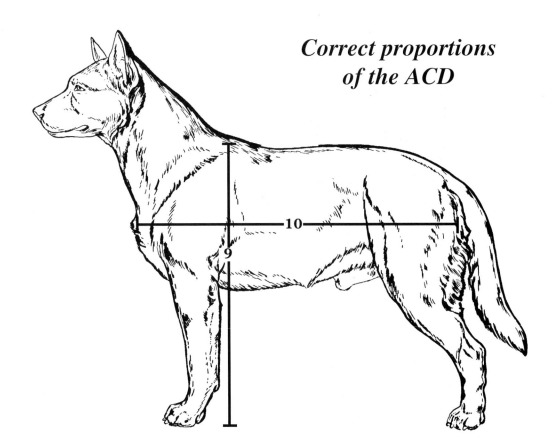

Correct proportions
of the ACD

The shoulder blades should slope well back, which allows the dog to take long, even strides. An upright shoulder results in short, stilted strides. For those who are not too good at geometry, or have difficulty visualising the angle of the shoulder blade, there is an easier, and sometimes more accurate way to decide. Simply watch the dog moving. If the dog is moving properly, the angle of the shoulder blade will be correct. After all, the only reason we worry about angle is to help us decide if the dog will move freely.

The rib cage must leave plenty of room for the heart and lungs, but if it is too wide (barrel ribbed) the elbows are pushed out which hinders movement. To allow for heart and lung space, without pushing the elbows out, the ribs should be deep as well as being well sprung. Also, they should continue well back towards the loins. Well sprung ribs do not dip behind the shoulder.

The level topline, referred to in show circles, is something of a misnomer. A glance at a lot of pictures of winning ACDs will show that none of them have geometrically level toplines. In all athletic breeds, the back rises over the loins and then slopes towards the root of the tail. The faster the breed, the more pronounced does this rise become, as in Greyhounds and Whippets.

The weakest part of any back, including our own, is the lumbar region – the bridge between the rib cage and the pelvis. It is well known that an arched bridge is stronger than a flat one, and that a

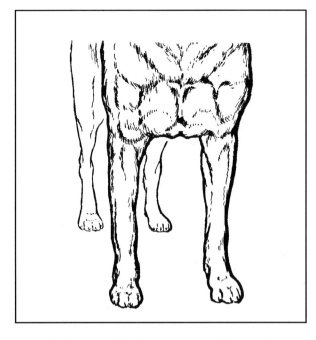

Correct forequarters: The chest should be deep and muscular, and moderately broad.

short bridge requires fewer supports than a long one, which is why a dog should be "strongly coupled". Apart from the added strength from a slightly curved spine, the loins should also carry a lot of very strong muscle. This adds to the overall impression of a curve over the loins.

Few people seem to realise how much a dog uses its back when galloping. With each stride, the back curves right round to a half-circle when the dog is off the ground. As the feet reach the ground, the half-circle is released and, like a coiled spring, the back straightens out. That is why animals like weasels and ferrets, with long backs and tiny legs, can run so fast. They use their backs to compensate for the shortness of leg. To go even further, a caterpillar, with no legs at all, only feet, propels itself along by arching the whole body and then flattening it out.

Not only must the ACD to be able to gallop – much faster than you might imagine – the dog also has to be able to duck and swerve at great speed. Many working breeds have to be athletic, but none more so than the working cattle dog. A weak back renders it useless. If you press down with the hands on the loins of a strong back, it will resist the pressure. In fact, some dogs will push up against the pressure. If you push down on a flat back, which some would regard as a level topline, it will sag because it is weak.

The hindquarters, too, are all important. There are no "front-wheel drives" in the animal world. A dog, a horse, or nearly any other four-legged vertebrate drives itself forward from behind. So the hindquarters should be very strong, with all the muscles well developed. Looking at the whole dog, most of the weight should appear to be towards the back end.

While the hindquarters provide the driving force, the forequarters provide the shock absorbers. The galloping dog propels its whole body off the ground with the hindquarters; it then reaches out with its front feet, which take the weight of the whole dog as they strike the ground. The shock is absorbed firstly by the large central pad, which should be like a piece of firm rubber. Next comes the pastern, which must be strong, slightly sloping and of medium length. If it is short and straight, there will be no "give" in it, but if it is long and slopes too much, it will be weak. From there, the shock goes up the arm and is absorbed by the joints and muscles of the elbows and shoulders. Those who have ridden different horses over fences know that one with straight shoulders is more likely to "peck", or even fall on landing, than one with good shoulders which reaches right forward with its forelegs, and lands smoothly without jarring.

FEET

The feet are well described. The old adage about 'no foot, no horse' is equally true of working dogs. Long hours working on a gravel road or rocky terrain, not to mention Australia's 'bindyi' could result in bleeding pads. (The bindyi is a creeping plant which covers large areas of Australia. It grows close to the ground and has spikes, rather like gorse.) When this happens the most perfect conformation according to the Standard will not help at all – that is on top of the need for the pads to act as shock absorbers for the whole body.

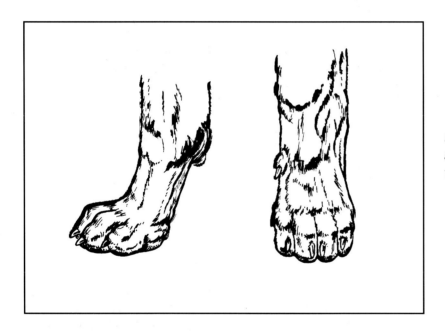

The feet should be round and the toes short, strong and well-arched.

This might be an appropriate point to mention that no part of the dog's anatomy is more affected by exercise than the feet and pasterns. We have seen flat and weak pasterns change beyond recognition after a period of regular exercise. When in training, racing Greyhounds are regularly weighed and measured. A dog which has been "resting" can increase in height by as much as an inch by the time it is fit.

TAIL

The tail is also well described. It should not be regarded simply as an appendage which enhances the appearance of the dog. It is generally accepted that the tail acts as a rudder and enables the dog to turn quickly. From considerable experience of Pembroke Welsh Corgis (in the days when they had legs!), we never found that the lack of a tail was a handicap in any way. This seems to be proved by the Stumpy Tailed Cattle Dog.

We believe that the tail, along with the eyes, are a guide to a dog's character. We also believe that the fetish for low tail carriage in some breeds is, at least partly, responsible for a deterioration of temperament. It is natural for a mature male dog to "wave his flag" while in the presence of other males. This does not mean that he necessarily wants to fight, just that he is telling the other males that he is as good as or better than they are.

Many dogs which carry their tails low simply do not have the guts to put them up. The Standard

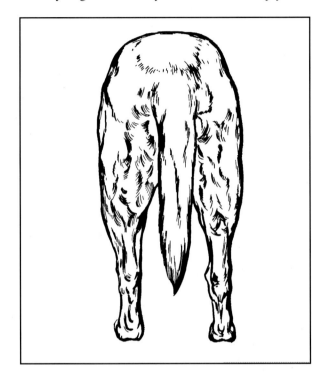

Correct hindquarters: The set-on of the tail is low, following the contours of the sloping rump.

allows the tail to be carried quite high – "to a vertical line drawn through the root." Some tails are carried beyond this point, but they are usually set on too high, which shortens the croup and detracts from the powerful hindquarters. We are told that the tail may be raised "during movement or excitement", but no mention is made of when the dog is working. Sheepdogs and cattle dogs which carry their tails high when working are usually headstrong, erratic workers.

MOVEMENT
Not surprisingly, the clause on gait/movement is the longest in the whole Standard, and it certainly is "of paramount importance." In the confines of the show ring, it is impossible to tell if a dog can gallop, turn and twist. But the average Cattle Dog working on a ranch or cattle station probably spends more time trotting behind a horse than actually working cattle. It is possible to get a fair idea in the show ring as to whether the dog is capable of doing that. But only if the dog is moved at the pace that would be necessary to keep up with a horse – a slow trot for the horse, but quite a fast one for the dog.

Incredible as it may seem, John has twice been asked to *walk* an ACD in the show ring! In both instances, this was by two of the best-known British All Rounders, who have judged many breeds all over the world. Not only is it necessary for the dog to move with a long, free stride, it must also give the impression of agility and be light on its feet. In proportion to its size, a Shire Horse probably takes a longer stride than a Polo Pony, but it wouldn't be much good at playing polo.

COLOUR
Coat is well defined in the Standard, but it is surprising how many writers claim that colour is clearly described. The only part which is clear to us, is the description of permissible tan markings on the blues. Blue could be slate-blue like a Great Dane, or one of the Kelpie's seven permissible colours, although this does not seem to be what is intended.

In the ACD blue is a mixture of black hairs and white ones, and the shade of blue varies from light to dark, according to the ratio of black to white hairs. The *Concise Oxford Dictionary* describes mottle as "irregular arrangement of spots or confluent blotches of colour", while the *Readers Digest Dictionary* describes it as "A spot of colour or shading contrasting with the rest of the surface on which it is found." Speckle is described in the *Concise Oxford Dictionary* as "A small spot or stain, especially one of the many irregular natural markings of skin etc." and in the *Readers Digest Dictionary* as "A speck or small spot: especially a natural dot of colour occurring in large numbers on skin, plumage or foliage." So you can take your pick.

There seems to be no real difference between speckle and mottle, and none of the descriptions say whether there should be light spots on a dark background, or dark spots on a light background.

The great variation in colour throughout the breed suggests that little attention has been paid to this point. 'A good dog cannot be a bad colour' seems to have been the maxim. In the first Standard, Kaleski was somewhat vague about colour. The head could be black or red, and the body dark blue on the back (sometimes with black saddle)."Light blue, sometimes mottled with white hairs on underpart of body" – that is the only reference to mottling he makes in the Standard; but in *Barkers and Biters* he refers to both blue and red speckle. The book has five pictures of Kaleski's own dogs, all of them referred to as "blue speckles", and apparently quite heavily speckled. None show the slightest sign of being dark on the back, with or without a black saddle.

The Australian Standard says that the blues have to be "blue, blue mottled or blue speckled", but the reds have to be a "good even red speckle all over". The American Standard states that blues

COLOUR
VARIATIONS

Lux. Ch. Damaran Dinga's Red Zoe, World Champion Spain 1992: Example of light-red speckle.

Quickneels Rusty Nail: A much darker red – note the dark muzzle.

Aust. Ch. Kombinalong Super K: Dark blue with rich tan markings.

Aust. Ch. Turrella Blue Lacy: Described as blue mottle – dark blue spots on a white background.

Am. Can. Ch. Tallawong Levi: Blue speckle, white flecks on a blue background.

Mikron.

can only be "blue or mottled", while the reds have to be "red speckled all over'" as in the Australian Standard.

Many top winning ACDs of both colours are neither speckled nor mottled, according to the descriptions in the dictionaries. Just as blue is a mixture of black and white hairs, so red is a mixture of red and white hairs, producing what is called 'roan' or 'sorrel' in a horse. The shade depends on the proportion of red to white hairs, as well as the shade of red hairs. But unlike the blues which can be blue, the reds must be speckled.

Some blues in Australia are virtually black and tan; one imported to the UK was described as such on its pedigree. Some people say this is due to continually breeding blue to blue. However, when breeders go to extremes, there are always others who go to opposite extremes. There are now breeders striving to produce light-coloured blues, which could end up like Dalmatians.

In an effort to clarify the situation, we wrote to the ANKC, but the reply was very ambiguous. However, the information they gave us, combined with captions on some of the photos we have received during the preparation of this book, suggests that mottled means dark spots on a light background, while speckled is light spots on a dark background.

White isn't mentioned in the Standard, but we have seen a whole litter with white markings, one with a huge patch on its side. If these were black or red they would be "undesirable", but apparently a judge is left to use his own discretion if they are white. Many ACDs – probably the majority – have a white stripe on the forehead, which is called a 'Bentley mark', because it is supposed to have been inherited from a very famous dog of that name. But while it is a feature of the breed, we are not told whether white is desirable or undesirable. The same applies to white rings or a black spot on the tail, both unique features of the breed.

Colour is by no means the most important factor in the ACD make-up. On the other hand, speckling or mottling – whichever you care to call it – is unique, irrespective of whether there are light spots on a dark background, or vice versa. It seems to be a great pity when a unique feature of any breed is lost. For that reason, we would like the Standard to give us much clearer information.

SIZE

With the Standard giving us a two-inch variation in height, there should be no problem keeping within the limits. But it *is* important to keep within those limits, and there may be something to be said for the Canadian idea of disqualifying animals more than half an inch under or over. When John attended the Cattle Working Trials in Tulsa, Oklahoma, it was noticeable that the smaller bitches were among the best workers, and several of these bitches were equally successful in the conformation classes the following day.

SUMMARY

Important as the points of the Standard are in themselves, it is much more important that they can all be fitted together like a jigsaw puzzle to produce a whole dog. Instead of evaluating the whole dog, some judges divide the animal up into sections and appear to have difficulty in deciding the relative importance of each section. It takes experience to differentiate between a good mover and an exceptional one, or to be sure that the expression and ear carriage are correct for the breed. But any fool can see a black patch on a dog's side, or a tail that is carried beyond the perpendicular. That is why a good dog, with an obvious fault, is sometimes placed below an inferior one with no such fault. The sentence under 'Faults' near the end of the Standard should always be borne in mind: "Any departure from the foregoing points should be considered a fault, and the seriousness with which the fault should be regarded should be in *exact proportion to its degree.*"

On becoming show dogs, many working breeds have been changed beyond all recognition and are quite incapable of carrying out their original task. Breeders are usually blamed for this, but it is really the judges who are to blame. If you are an exhibitor you will not please all the judges all of the time, but unless you please some of the judges some of the time, you might as well give up. If the judge likes a freak, as some judges appear to do, and you want to win, then you have to produce a freak. This has not happened to our breed – not yet!

People we know in Australia, who are dependent on dogs to help on cattle stations, are very scathing of the ACDs of the show ring. They are too short in the leg and too heavy and clumsy, they say. They tell us that the majority of dogs working cattle in Australia are ACDs crossed with Border Collies or Kelpies. There has always been a tendency among working dog men to believe that any dog which has ever entered a show ring must be quite useless as a worker. Well over a century ago a type of dog was developed to do a very difficult job. That type has changed remarkably little – much less so than many other working breeds. It provides a positive and stable ideal at which breeders and judges can aim.

Only a very small percentage of ACDs bred today ever work cattle, but that is no reason why they should not be capable of doing so. In the USA and Canada, stock dog trials for a wide variety of breeds have become extremely popular in recent years. The AKC now offers official titles for herding dogs. The very first dog to qualify HX (Herding Excellent) on cattle was the ACD Ch. Buzzards Red Tubs – and he did it when he was eleven years old, by which time he had sired over fifty Champions in the show ring. Sadly Tubs, who spent most of his time working cattle on owner Jim Buzzard's ranch in Oklahoma, died in March 1992 at the age of thirteen. It is most encouraging to note how many breeders are successful in the show ring and in cattle working trials with the same dogs.

The ACD is a special breed to the Australians. 'Yippee', owned by Loraine Teston, posing in a clothing advertisement in the 'Dolly Magazine'.
Tony Duran.

Chapter Three

THE ACD IN AUSTRALIA

The ACD has been part of Australian history for the past one hundred and fifty years. The history of the breed has been fully covered in a previous chapter, but long before the Australian National Kennel Club decided to call the breed the Australian Cattle Dog, it was known far and wide as Halls Heelers, Blue Heelers or Queensland Heelers – the drover's dog and guard dog which has no equal.

The ACD still holds a special place in the heart of the Australian public. When there was a special issue of stamps in the eighties, one of the four dogs featured was the ACD; then there is the famous 'Blue Heeler Bridge' in New South Wales. The first bridge, built in 1870 at a cost of £75, was washed away by floods, as was the second. The third bridge, costing $78,000, was opened in 1976. The pioneers of the breed are not forgotten, and The Australian Cattle Dog Society of NSW presented a large bronze plaque to commemorate Thomas Hall, whose breeding experiments in the 1840s laid the foundation of the breed.

THE ACD AS A SHOW DOG

Although bred from the mid 19th Century onwards to work stock and guard property, it was not long before the settlers started to show their dogs along with other stock at local Agricultural Shows. In the early 20th Century, Kaleski relates that dairy farmers would often want to buy a dog for both work and show, offering as little as £2! But the price of a good working dog, with show potential, would have been about £12.

Registrations reached a peak of 4,278 in 1988, dropping to 2,870 in 1991, but still maintaining the second highest number of registrations in the Working Group. For over forty years there have been complaints that the ACD was often overlooked in all breed shows. Writing in 1987, W. D. Crawley, who has attended over eighty 'Royals' during his career in the dog world, said that ACDs were then at their highest level since the 1950-60 era – although he did consider that, with a few notable exceptions, handlers could take a tip on presentation from some other breeds!

In the 1950s two of the outstanding dogs were Ch. Little Logic and his son Ch. Logic's Return. A great number of present-day dogs are descended from these two well-known winners. Two other winners from that 'golden era', as it was called, were Ch. Hillside Duke and Ch. Trueblue patches. Duke was awarded two Best in Show awards by the late Roy Burnell. This was very unusual at the time, but Roy was a judge who had a very good eye for a dog and the courage to put up a good one. The only criticism of these dogs was that they were very dark, almost black, but they did have rich tan markings. Today's dogs still tend to be very dark and, unfortunately, a lot of very light tan, almost fawn or cream, markings have crept in.

Ch. Wooleston Blue Jock: Best of Breed at the Sydney Royal, 1967. Owned by Bernie and Berenice Walters.

Ch. Wooleston Blue Jennie 1973, a Champion in the show ring, who worked sheep and cattle. She was the foundation bitch of the Tallawong kennel. Bred by Bernie and Berenice Walters. Owned by Ken and Helen Dickson.

Barkleigh-Shute.

LEADING BREEDERS

The Wooleston kennels of Bernie and Berenice Walters have figured largely on the ACD scene for many years, and Wooleston dogs have set many a new breeder on the road to success in Australia, and in other countries round the world. In 1967 the beautifully speckled blue dog, Ch. Wooleston Blue Jock, was Best of Breed at the Sydney Royal when one hundred and fifty ACDs were exhibited. Ch. Wooleston Blue Joka, a well-known winner in the seventies was a son of Am. Ch. Wooleston Blue Jester, exported to Bonnie Fischer in 1975. Other Wooleston exports have become

Ch. Tallawong Blue Jack, pictured at sixteen months of age. He was Best Opposite Sex at the Sydney Royal in 1974.

1975 Ch. Tallawong Blue Jeff: sire of six Australian Champions.

Barkleigh-Shute.

Champions in different countries, such as Sweden and Holland.

Ken and Helen Dickson of the famous Tallawong prefix were delighted when they bought the bitch puppy, Wooleston Blue Jenny, in 1967. Jenny, who quickly became a Champion, was an outstanding bitch who worked sheep and cattle from an early age. Apart from her own show career, she was also an excellent brood bitch. She won the Bitch Challenge at the Adelaide Royal in 1970 and 1971.

Among the numerous winners from this kennel, some will never be forgotten. A son of Jenny,

Ch. Tallawong Blue Jacinta with her daughter Tallawong Blue Jinnnie, and three granddaughters, Tallawong Blue Janome, Ch. Tallawong Blue Jeffelle and Ch. Tallawong Blue Jezelda. Bred and owned by Ken and Helen Dickson.   *Barkleigh-Shute.*

1976 Ch. Landmaster U'Sundowner, sired by Ch. Galwarri Red Flare. The highest awarded red ACD in Australia for many years, and sire of many Champions. Bred and owned by Connie Redhead.

ABOVE LEFT: Ch. Landmaster Showdancer, another successful Ch. Landmaster U'Sundowner son. Bred and owned by Connie Redhead.   C. S. Photography.

ABOVE: Ch. Landmaster U'Show Off, owned and bred by Connie Redhead.

ABOVE: 1975 Ch. Taitsglen Red Sonny: Multiple winner, owned by A. and C. Edwards.

RIGHT: Ch. Turrella Red Cindy (Turrella Double Duke – Whitefence Red Cinder): Multiple winner, including Best in Show ACD Society, New South Wales, 1987. Bred and owned by A. and C. Edwards.

Ch. Justoz Blue Jess, owned by Ray Sykes.

Ch. Tallawong Blue Jack, was Best Opposite Sex in Show at Sydney Royal in 1974 under the distinguished all rounder, the late Thelma Gray (UK). A grandson of Jenny, Ch. Tallawong Blue Jeff, ran up an impressive number of wins with a record twenty challenges in five States. As a sire he was equally well-known, siring six Australian Champions.

In Western Australia the Baiamul prefix of Roberta and Kevin Thorn is well-known in the show ring, although fifty per cent of pups bred are sold for work with stock. Ch. Baiamul Blue Otto (Ch. Baiamul Blue Xerxes – Baiamul Blue Yana) had the honour of going Best in Show all breeds, at the Perth Royal in 1987 – the first ACD to do so. The Baiamul ACDs have been exported to several countries, including the US and the UK, where they have done a considerable amount of winning.

All the dogs mentioned so far have been blues, but in 1970 Bob and Connie Redhead started their Landmaster kennels. In 1979 their red bitch, Landmaster Darling Red, won the bitch Challenge at the Adelaide Royal. She soon became a Champion and was exported to the UK in January 1980. Perhaps the best-known Landmaster dog was Ch. Landmaster U'Sundowner, another red. By Ch. Galwarri Red Flare out of Ch. Lenthel Flaming Star. 'Sunny' won seventeen Best in Show awards (all breeds) and thirty-two Best Exhibit in Group. He won the Dog Challenge at the Adelaide Royal in 1984 and 1986 (his sons, Ch. Landmaster Sundancer and Ch. Landmaster Showdancer, winning it in 1985 and 1987). Sunny was a great character, and an even greater showman – ably assisted by Connie. He sired numerous winners, many going overseas to found ACD kennels in the UK, US, Sweden and other countries. But he was also a much-loved and loyal companion to Bob and Connie and their children.

In Queensland, Ch. Plowman Blue Buckaroo, bred by Philip Pearce, and now owned by Pat French, is another notable dog. Sired by Ch. Greeben Hobbs O Hell out of Doolagarl Miss Silver, this dog had produced ten Champion offspring by mid-1989. Amongst 'Boy's' many wins was a

Reserve Best in Show all breeds at Townsville. His daughter, Ch. Plowman Georgie Girl, is also a big winner.

In Victoria, Phil Morrison is currently having a lot of success with his home-bred blue dog, Binshaws Swaggie Jack (Ch. Binshaw Blue Banjo – Walgee Blue Brooke). Jack is totting up an impressive number of wins.

R. and E. Cook's Rokeglen ACDs have been exported worldwide, winning successfully for their new owners. American Ch. Rokeglen Blue Phantom, belonging to Jim Buzzard of Vinita, was the top producer of ACDs at only two years old. 'Mr T', as he is known, also works regularly on Jim's ranch.

THE SHOW SCENE

Dog Shows are very popular in Australia, and in most States specialist and all breed shows are held every weekend. The smaller shows tend to be rather informal affairs, often held in City parks. Exhibitors and their families arrive for a day out, complete with dogs, dog crates, umbrellas and picnics.

Rules for showing dogs vary from State to State. Each State has its own Canine Association, but the Australian National Kennel Council is there to promote canine interests and to co-ordinate and standardise procedures. Puppies are shown as young as three months, but a dog must be six months old before becoming a Champion.

To achieve Championship status, a dog must win a hundred points, which are gained when winning Challenge Certificates. The number of points varies according to the size of the class, and the type of show. No dog may gain more than twenty points at any one show. Each State has a 'Royal' every year. These are very prestigious Agricultural Shows which last several days, and they have a large Dog Show section. A win at one of the Royals is a very coveted award. Unlike

Ch. Walgee Blue Clancy (Ch. Tallawong Blue Jack – Ch. Tallawong Blue Jefelle): Challenge Dog and Best of Breed at the Melbourne Royal, 1988-89. Bred and owned by Peter and Gail Ferguson.

Twigg.

Ch. Binshaw Swaggie Jack (Ch. Binshaw Blue Banjo – Ch. Walgee Blue Brooke), bred and owned by Phil and C. Morison. Jack won his title at twelve months, and is one of the up-and-coming dogs of the nineties.

Twigg.

the smaller shows, the dogs at the Royals are benched. There are six Groups, and the ACD is in the Working Group.

WORKING AND OBEDIENCE
Unlike many European countries, notably Scandinavia, where Working Tests are mandatory before a dog becomes a Champion, Australia has no Working Trials for ACDs. This is rather sad as the breed was bred specifically to work cattle in that country. It seems that the number of pure ACDs working stock is falling. Most of the cattle dogs, we are told by Kent Lithgow (son of Scott Lithgow, author of *Training and Working Dogs*) are now ACD cross, either Border Collie or Kelpie – a cross which seems to combine the best of both breeds, but Kent does lament that it is getting more and more difficult to find the right type of working dogs.

For some time there has been a movement to establish some form of 'stock assessment', rather on the lines of the US Herding Trials, but so far nothing has come of it. ACDs can, and do, hold their own in Obedience. The Australian titles are CD and CDX (Companion Dog and Companion Dog Excellent); UD and UDX (Utility Dog); TD and TDX (Tracking dog). Because of the summer heat, Tracking trials are only run from March to September, and as only very few Tracking trials are run in this short season, it is very difficult for handlers to qualify their dogs. Obedience Champions do not gain their titles on points, but on qualifications won. In NSW dogs must gain a CD, CDX, UD, TD, and TDX in order to become an Obedience Champion.

Loraine Teston, breeder and trainer of the Rewuri ACDs, has done extremely well in Obedience, and also does a fair amount of film and advertising work with her dogs. One of the most famous Obedience dogs was Beronganella Robyn UD, TD. 'Birra-li' is the founder of a long line of Obedience dogs – her descendants in direct line, having amassed a total of twelve Obedience titles between them. The top Obedience ACD in 1992 is Rewuri Blue Chipala UD, owned and trained

Beronganella Robyn UD TD, known as 'Birra-Li' owned and trained by Loraine Teston.

'Birra-Li at the starting flag at a Tracking Trial.

Rewuri Blue Chipala UD: Top Obedience ACD in NSW 1991-92, showing his scent discrimination skills. Owned and trained by Alfreda O'Brien.

Tangui King Khan CDX AD, competing in Agility. Owned by B. and V. Cliff.

by Alfreda O'Brien. Chipala has won the Birra-Li Award for the third time. This award was presented by Loraine Teston in memory of her bitch, and to encourage people to compete in Obedience.

The Rewuri dogs are not worked on stock by their owner, but Loraine does use good working strains when breeding. The sire of Rewuri Mikibri, now winning show classes and Obedience in Sweden, was Ch. Lawnville Supreme, who is the fifth generation of Champions working on properties.

Australia is a vast continent and it has not been easy to gather as much information as we would have wished. But we have done our best to touch on the most salient points concerning the breed and to give a cross- section of famous dogs, both past and present. Many breeders worldwide have reason to be grateful that they were given the chance to start their own kennels of ACDs with good, sound stock from Australia.

Chapter Four

THE ACD IN NORTH AMERICA

ESTABLISHING THE BREED

Australian Cattle Dogs had been in the US for some years when two enthusiasts, Christina Risk and Esther Ekman, met up at a dog show. They decided they would try to form a club for the breed and held a meeting in early 1967. A little later they formed a club called the Queensland Heeler Club of America. But when the American Kennel Club explained to them that a Parent Club must use the name under which the breed was shown in both America and Australia, the name was changed to The Australian Cattle Dog Club of America. This club came into being in February 1969, with Christina Risk (Smith) as President and Program Director.

The Club and the Breed Registry grew steadily throughout the seventies, and the first Specialty Fun Match was held in Calistoga in 1976. The breed gained official recognition in the AKC Stud books in May 1980, and ACDs were then allowed to be shown in regular breed classes in AKC Licenced shows.

In 1984 the Club held the first AKC Licenced Breed and Obedience Independent Specialty Show for Australian Cattle Dogs. Since that time Conventions with Specialty and Obedience Shows and Versatility events have been held annually (AKC Herding Trials have now replaced the Versatility). In 1980 1,685 ACDs were registered with the AKC. From 1981 to 1986 the numbers dropped to between 500 and 800 a year, rising in 1987 to 1,048, and in 1991 to 1,433.

Right from the start, the breed has done well in Obedience. The first recorded ACD to win an Obedience title was the import, Glen Iris Boomerang, owned by Carol Mork of California. 'Frosty', as he was known, qualified for his CD in May 1965, and later gained his CDX. Frosty was an excellent worker with eight High in Trials, and once scored 199 1/2 out of a possible 200 at the Golden Gate KC Show in 1967. The first Obedience Trial Champion was Helen Brigham's OTCH Katrina Piglet Roo TD. 'Kate' became a Champion in 1983. Another early Obedience enthusiast was Barbara Taylor; her Mitchell's Tina Marie UD was the first ACD in the world to obtain a Utility Degree.

TYPES OF SHOW

The AKC has three types of shows: All-breed, Specialty, and Sanctioned Matches. Specialty shows are run by a club or society of one particular breed. Specialties are very social affairs, with exhibitors and their families and dogs often taking over a large hotel complex and camping ground. As well as show classes they often put on Junior Showmanship, Sweepstakes, Herding clinics and Trials, Obedience instruction classes, and sometimes Agility and Flyball.

It is both interesting and encouraging to see how many top winning show dogs also compete –

Mex. Can. Am. Ch. Silverhills Goin Up N'Smoke (Ch. Bushrangers Crossfire – Silverhills Red Pepper) BOB ACDC of Canada National Specialty, 1989 and 1990. Bred by Kim Eberley, owned by Gina McDonnel.

and win – in Herding and Obedience, etc. In 1988 Violet Tipping's Can. Ch. Silent Partn'r AJ Maleri CD was Winning Bitch and Herding Trial Winner at the Tulsa Specialty.

BECOMING A CHAMPION
In the US show winners of each class compete against each other for Winners Dog or Winners Bitch. This award wins points towards the Champion title. The Winners Dog and Winners Bitch compete against Champions present for Best of Breed.

To become a Champion a dog must gain fifteen points, six of which have to be won at two different shows under two different judges. The rest of the points must be won under at least one more judge. The number of points given per show varies according to a scale based on the number of dogs actually defeated in a given breed. The maximum number of points that can be earned at any one show is five.

LEADING ACDs
Last year 10,574 events were held under AKC rules. Over 6,000 of these were licenced-member dog club shows, Obedience, Herding, Field Trials, and Hunting events, at which Championship points could be won. With that number of shows and the vast distances involved, it is obviously only possible to mention a few well-known dogs.

Going back a few years to the late seventies, Ch. Fischer Streak Bingo (Cherimoya Blue Streak – Fischer's Miss Kiko) helped to lay the foundation of the Fischer, Heelerhill and Imbach ACDs. Bred by Bonnie Fischer, 'Bingo' was BISS of the 1977 ACDCA Specialty Fun Match at Luverne. Among many other winners, he was the sire of Ch. Frog Acres Bingo Blue Jasper CD, VQW, the 1985 ACDCA BISS, and grandsire of Ch. Imbachs Paddy Willie, the 1991 ACDCA BISS.

Ch. Hoosier Snicker Trooper Dan (Brasco Snicker Doodle Dandy – Hoosier Snicker's Missy), owned by Roger and Gayle Beers, is now fourteen years old, and still "as arrogant and aristocratic as ever", according to Gayle! Sire of multiple Champions, he was the sire of Ch. Brasco Easy Rider and Ch. Brasco Blue Destiny CD – both ACDCA National Specialty Match Best of Breed winners. He also sired Ch. Brasco Bobbi Sue O'Tailwind, BOS at the first ACDCA AKC Licensed show, held in St Charles. Bobbi Sue and Easy Rider were littermates.

Another winner in both the show ring and Obedience in the eighties was Ch. Rotom's Wily Blue Willie CDX, VQW (Mywumble Blue Stockman – Ch. Pavesi Kandi Dinki Di). Owned by Lisa and Dub Perkins. 'Willie' was High Scoring Obedience Dog 1984 ACDCA National Specialty Show.

Currently, Wilma Dame's Ch. Buckeye's Waltzing Matilda, bred by Glenna Dickerson is the 'most titled' ACD in the country. Her titles include: Champion, TT, Am. & Can. UD-TDX, UKC-CDX, SKC-CD, Herding: AVQW, Std-C, HIC, FBX (Flyball Dog Excellent), CGC (Canine Good Citizen) and Agility Dog. Matti is by Ch. Yambungan Nullabor Red out of Ch. Buckeye's First Lady Zsa Zsa. At ten years of age, 'Matti' is now running for her second Agility Title.

In 1983 Ch. Bryn Mawr's Razzle Dazzle CD, bred by Pete and Donna Ellis and owned by Carol Vohsen, was and *is* the *only* bitch to go BIS at an All Breeds Show. Still on 'firsts', Ch. Buzzards Finders Keepers (Ch. Rokeglen Phantom – Buzzards Red Foxy), bred by Jim Buzzard and owned by John and Cheryl Kurpass, was the first bitch, and the first red, to attain the honour of being BISS since AKC Licensing. This was at the Florida Specialty in 1990.

A fairly recent import is Roger and Gayle Beers' Ch. Doolgarl Wonder Miss (Plowman Blue Buckaroo – Doolagarl Fancy Miss). 'Bonnie' quickly justified their choice by going Best of Winners at the Florida Specialty in 1991. Another winning Brasco is Ch. Brasco Bold N' Brawn

Am. Ch. Brasco Bobbi Sue O'Tailwind: BOS at the first ACDCA AKC Licensed Show. Owned by J. Elliath.

John L. Ashbey.

Am. Ch. Brasco Bold N' Brawn: Winners Dog 1991 ACDCA National Specialty. Owned by J. and L. Broade.

Downey Photography.

(Ch. Brasco Gotcha A Scramlin – Brasco Just Fine and Jandy) A very typical ACD, with the good temperament associated with this kennel, 'Brawny' has notched up an impressive number of wins.

At the 1992 National Specialty, which drew an entry of 148, Winners Dog was Tim Demoulin's Heelerhill Billy The Kid. RWD was Roy and Sandy Darnell's Whiskey River Cattle Baron (Cattlenip Red Collarenebri – Buzzards Lady in Red Too) who was made up to Champion at that show. Winners Bitch was Judy Van Straten's Dancer's Angel in Disguise, and RWB was Frank Deppo and Cheryl Head's Crown G Blue Adaliad. The judge, Mr Forsyth, selected Ch. Mtn Grown in Like Flint as BISS. Ch. Bryn Mawr's Rough and Rowdy won the Publicity Award for the Sire of most Champions, the bitch award going to Ch. Mtn Grown Annie Oakley. Another top producer is Buzzards Blue Nig (Powr-Pak Super Blue – Dixie), bred by Amos Stidham. 'Nig' has,

Am. Can. Ch. Doolagarl Blue Charm (BOS ACDC of Canada 1990, and only ACD bitch to win a Group in Canada), her daughter, Bushrangers N'Silverhills Lea (Winners Bitch ACDC of Canada 1990), and her son, Am. Can. Ch. Bushrangers Stand By Me (Winners Dog ACDC of America 1990). Owned by Kim Eberley.   *Mikron Photos.*

Am. Ch. Kriegers Dandy Lion, owned by Larry Hooper.

Chuck Tatham.

Am. Can Ch. Silver Hills Angela HC QW (Am. Ch. Silverhills Nugget – Silverhills Sonya) Veteran Bitch 1990 and 1991. Bred by Helen Blankers, owned by Kim Eberley.

Mikron Photos.

Am. Can. Ch. Whiskey River Cattle Baron (Cattlenip Red Collarenebri – Buzzards Lady in Red Two): Reserve Winners Dog 1992 ACDC National Specialty. Handled by Max L. Spears.

Rich Bergman.

so far, produced sixteen Champions. The 1991 Publicity award for Top ACD – Breed points, Dog and Overall – went to Pat Imbach's Ch. Imbach's Paddy Willy. At the 1992 annual banquet Pat Imbach was honoured by the ACDCA when she received the Gaines Award for Good Sportsmanship. Pat is a tireless worker for the good of the ACD, and this was a very popular and well-deserved award. With her husband Bill, they run a ranch in Northern California, raising beef cattle and ACDs.

No book on the ACD would be complete without a mention of Jim and Sue Buzzard's great dog, Champion Red Tubs HX (Scobie Rae Cricket – Buzzards Blue Hart). Born in 1979, this remarkable dog won his Championship title when he was four years old – going straight into the ring from the back of a truck! He won the HIS Gold Certificate of Distinction for siring over fifty Champions. At the age of eleven, he was the first dog – of any breed – to gain the AKC Herding Excellent Title, his first two qualifying scores having been earned at the first AKC Trial ever held.

'Tubs' lived most of his working life on his owner's ranch in Oklahoma. He often helped out at

Am. Ch. Buzzards Red Tubs HX, working cattle at the 1990 ACDC National Specialty when he was eleven years old. Bred and owned by Jim Buzzard. *Lori Herbel.*

cattle shows in the Mid West, where he won a lot of admiration from spectators when he was following stock out to the wash or tie out areas. Even the 'great' have their weaknesses, and maybe in 'Tub's' case it was food! There is a rumour that he once helped himself to a small girl's hot dog, as she carelessly dangled it from her hand at a show. On another occasion, at a Fair, he came across a bag of donuts and carefully carried it home for breakfast!

THE VERSATILE ACD
Americans have been careful to import from some of the best kennels in Australia, including Rokeglen, Tallawong, Landmaster, Baiamul, Wooleston and many more. The result can be seen in the breed as it is today. America has always been called the Land of Opportunity – and with its well-deserved reputation for versatility, it is little wonder that the ACD is proving increasingly popular. The list of activities in which they take part is quite staggering.

A red dog from Rescue is now working for the Customs Service at Kennedy Airport, making a successful job of drug detection. Several ACDs are doing the same job at Miami and Los Angeles airports. A well-known winning dog doing a real job of work is Ch. Wagga Wagga Blue Ace CD. Ace was awarded the ACDCA 1991-2 Hero Dog of the Year Award. Ace was accepted into the K9 Police Dog Training Program, and partnered with Officer Tom Murdoch; he is now a fully fledged working street Policedog. With Tom, he was part of one of the three winning teams to win an award at the Officers Banquet at Mountain Democrat in 1992. A number of ACDs are enjoying Schutzhund work. George Krohn of Cleveland, Ohio, is proud of his dog, Buzzards Out of The Blue: 'Corky' is the first ACD ever to receive a Schutzhund title in the USA.

Apart from regularly working both sheep and cattle, there is an ACD in Alaska working for the Department of Fish and Wildlife, herding Muskox. A number are working as Therapy Dogs (similar to the UK Pat Dogs), and as Hearing Impaired Dogs (similar to UK Hearing Dogs for the Deaf). Quite a number are active with Search and Rescue teams. On the lighter side, we have heard of some that enjoy Lure Racing, act as Sled Dogs, and one that helps his enterprising young owner deliver the morning papers.

CANADA

It was in the 1950s and 1960s that the ACD became known in Canada, and people began to be interested in the breed's ability to work cattle. But it was not until 1979 that the breed was officially recognised by the Canadian Kennel Club. Previously it had been accepted by the CKC into the Miscellaneous Breeds Listing. Much credit for getting the breed recognised must go to Doreen Allen and Millie Pratt. The first ACD to be registered in 1979 was Dajacki Ringmaster, imported by Mrs Pratt and owned by J. B. Davis. From 1972 there had been an unofficial breed club, which was finally recognised by the CKC as The Australian Cattle Dog Club of Alberta in 1978. This was later to become the ACD Club of Canada.

In 1981 the club started holding Training Clinics (working cattle) to promote the breed as an all-round working dog. In 1983 members got together to draw up rules for future trials for Cattle Dogs working stock. These rules were submitted to the CKC the same year, which was a big step forward, as no other breed club, worldwide, had submitted a proposal for titles for dogs that work stock, to a national Kennel Club.

In 1985 the club held their first (unofficial) trial at Calgary and drew a good entry, Maggie Monical's Yambungan Cariboo Nutmeg winning the Open Cattle Trial. In 1984 the club held its first breed booster at an all-breed conformation show, the winner being Cattlenip A Tsetse Bit, owned by Sandra Kunzel. The first CKC Stockdog Trial was held in Alberta in 1989. Seven ACDs were entered, four already being Show Champions. There were four separate trials, the first being won by the ACD Cattlenip Bunya Blue QW, bred and owned by Dawn O'Reilly. Blue earned her SSC (Started Stockdog Certificate) title that day. Cassie Cady also won a SSC title with her eleven-year-old ACD, Can. Am. Ch. Yambungan Nullabor Red. Red was an experienced stock dog, having been brought up from a ranch in Montana for the trials. Altogether, five ACDs qualified that day.

Dawn O'Reilly originally started her Cattlenip kennels in Australia in 1965; she bred ACDs to provide workers to control her herd of registered Brahmas. She then became interested in the show side, but she has always bred stock that was dual purpose. She moved to Canada in 1977 with all her breeding stock, and then added to this with good imported youngsters. She did a great deal to get the ACD known in Canada, with many of her dogs, or progeny by her dogs, winning well in the show ring and trials.

A notable winner and sire was Am. Can. Ch. Cattlenip Heel Fly Red CD, VQW (Am. Can. Ch. Yambungan Nullabor Red – Am. Can. Ch. Masked Bandit of Pitjantjara). 'Red' was a lovely red speckle, a colour not seen as often as it should be. Unfortunately for Canada, Dawn returned to Australia in 1990. Before she left she was co-chairman of the CKC Stockdog Committee, member of the ACD Club of America Herding Committee, and the ACD Club of Canada Herding Committee, trial judge, instinct tester, and instructor for herding clinics in the US and Canada.

A well-known Canadian-bred and owned dog is Am. Can. Ch. Silent Partn'r A. J. Maleri CDX, SSC, Am CDX, VQW. In both 1988 and 1989 she was Am. Versatility Winner, Winners Bitch at the American National Specialty in 1988, and BOS at the Canadian Specialty in 1989. 'Mali' is by

Can. Ch. Yambungan Cariboo Nutmeg CD, QW, VQW (Cattlenip Tapper Lightly – Yambungan Jundah). Bred by Cheryl Scott, owned by Maggie Monical. 'Nutmeg' was purchased mainly as a ranch dog, a job she learned quickly and well.

Am. Can. Ch. Heel Fly Red CD, VQW out of Waters Blue Sally. The same year, yet another Canadian won the Advanced Versatility, this being Maggie Monical's Can. Ch. Yambungan Cariboo Nutmeg Can. CD, QW, VQW, while Bonnie Boe's Can. Ch. RT's Walalla Can. CD, VQW gained 100 per cent to win the Jackpot Cattle Penning, and went Reserve Winners Bitch – a year to remember for the Canadians!

The Canadian Herding Trials are different from the American version, but dogs compete in both regularly. The same goes for the Obedience Trials, but in this case they are very similar in both countries. Canada is a very large country, and the club is relatively small. However, there are a number of dogs working in Obedience, mostly to CD level. Probably the majority of the breed live on farms, but not all work stock, as many are kept as guard dogs. The Herding Sport is growing steadily, with many people attending clinics.

As a show dog, the ACD is not high in the popularity stakes, but this applies to other countries too. The ACD is, after all, a rugged workman-like dog, and many judges go for the type of dog that has spent the previous day in the beauty parlour!

Am. Can. Ch. Cattlenip Heel Fly Red CD, VQW (Am. Can. Ch. Yambungan Nullabor Red – Am. Can. Ch. Masked Bandit of Pitjantjara: Multiple Group and breed winner, and sire of winners. Owned by Dawn O'Reilly.

Can. Am. Ch. Silent Partn'r AJ Maleri CDX, SSC, Am. CDX, VQW (Am. Can. Ch. Cattlenip Heel Fly – Waters Blue Sally), owned by Violet Tipping.

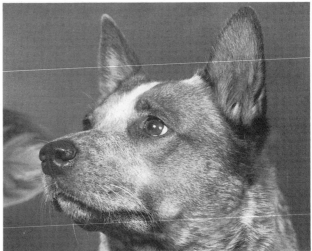

Can. Am. Ch. Silent Partn'r EJ Nikita and her son, Can. Ch. Quickheels Rhythm and Blues, owned by Meaghan Thacker.

Can. Ch. Vitips Downright Dusty (Can. Am. Ch. Bushrangers Licorice Sting – Can. Am. Ch. Silent Partn'r AJ Maleri CDX, SSC, Am CDX, VQW): Multiple Group and breed placer. Bred by Violet Tipping.

Some ACDs belong to a group called The Chilliwack Scramblers, which was formed to show the public that dogs can be good citizens. The team performs at various events from Chilliwack to Vancouver, giving Agility, Flyball and Obedience displays. It is very encouraging that so many of the Canadian dogs are dual purpose, and many other countries would do well if they followed suit.

Chapter Five

THE ACD WORLDWIDE

UNITED KINGDOM

THE FIRST IMPORTS

The first registered ACDs to arrive in the UK were the two blue puppies, Lenthel Flinton (Lenthel U'Tiga – Aust. Ch. Lenthel Jilliby) and Lenthel Darlot (Lenthel Urick – Lenthel Larro), bred by Len Carter of South Australia, and imported by Malcolm Dudding. With these two, the Swordstone Kennel was started. In early 1980 we imported Aust. Ch Landmaster Darling Red (Aust. Ch. Landmaster U'Sundowner – Rocambole Red Jody) in whelp to Aust. Ch. Landmaster Eureka (Aust. Ch. Wooleston Blue Jocka – NZ. & Aust. Ch. Landmaster Orion). Bred by Connie Redhead of South Australia, 'Honey' was to prove an outstanding brood bitch and a big winner in AVNSC classes in the UK.

In late 1980 we also imported Pwca Blue Boomerang (Dutch Ch. Edgirdee Happy Jackeroo – Dutch Ch. Wooleston Blue Camille). Bred by the Van Kloeke Evers of Holland, 'Jockey' was recommended to us by the late Harry Spira as a suitable dog to use on Honey. In 1981 Julie Horne of Kenya came to live in the UK and brought with her the ACD bitch, Olechuga Blue Maralinga.

There were no more imports until 1986 when two puppies arrived. Rob Marchant brought in Ravenswing Flint (Aust. Ch. Banjine Blue Tough – Colonydane Blue Shado), bred by J. Cornish of West Australia. Also from WA, we imported Baiamul Blue Dinkydi (Aust. Ch. Baiamul Blue Benjamin – Aust. Ch. Baiamul Blue Lara), bred by Roberta Thorn. In 1987 Stella Smyth went to Germany to collect Boomerang Blue Alberta (Can. Ch. Bluepine Rebels Rip – Yambungan Bunyip Blue), a two-year-old bred by the late Afra Hasper.

Next to arrive were two blue bitch pups, Rokeglen Blue Mankara (Rokeglen The Wayfarer – Valaviv Touch of Class) and Rokeglen Blue Tarlaga (Aust. Ch. Rokeglen Blue Taipan – Rokeglen Miss Mindi), from the well-known kennels of K. E. and R. Cook of New South Wales, imported by the Earl and Countess of Huntingdon; they also imported the blue dog Kristad Eureka Digger (Aust. Ch. Kristad Rebel King – Aust. Ch. Linklowe Jessie) from NSW in 1992.

THE GENE POOL IN THE UK

There are now just over two hundred ACDs in the UK, but it can be seen that with only eleven imports the gene pool is very limited. In the early years the breed, especially the reds, were very much of the same type and quality – a fact mentioned by the well-known Australian All Rounder, Bill Weston, who judged our first Open Show in 1987. Many of the imports, all of which have been blue, have been from completely different strains, resulting in considerable variation in type,

Aust. Ch. Landmaster Darling Red 1978 (Aust. Ch. Landmaster U'Sundowner – Rocambole Red Jody). Bred by Connie Redhead, imported by the authors in 1980.

Sally Anne Thompson.

Baiamul Blue Dinkydi of Formakin 1986 (Aust. Ch. Baiamul Blue Benjamin – Aust. Ch. Baiamul Blue Lara: Reserve Best in Show ACD Society of GB Open Show, 1992. Bred by R. Thorn, imported by the authors, 1986.

R. Willbie.

size etc., and with some of the blues becoming very dark. The Kennel Club has recently announced that it is to relax some of the rules concerning artificial insemination. There has also been a great improvement in the technology of freezing and storing semen, and in its transport. There are now four freezing centres in Australia, and it is probable, too, that in the foreseeable future there will be less stringent quarantine regulations. All of which could be a great help to breeders in this country.

THE ACD SOCIETY

In 1985 a meeting was held to discuss the formation of an ACD Society. This was organised by Carol Snell, who became the society's first secretary. In June of the same year the Kennel Club granted permission for the ACD Society of GB to be officially recognised. In 1986 Stella Smyth became secretary and has remained so since then. John was the first chairman, becoming president in 1990. In 1987 the ACD Society successfully held its first Open Show at Solihull, an event which is now held annually.

In 1990 it was decided to hold some form of behaviour tests for the breed. The first, fairly simple test was the Character Test. This test, carried out on the lead, is to ensure that the dog has a stable temperament, and can behave well in the presence of other dogs, children, strangers etc. The dog must not be nervous, and must be able to cope with heavy traffic, strange objects and noises. So far twelve dogs have passed this test.

The Good Companion Test may only be taken after a pass in the Character Test. In this test the dogs have to retrieve, pass other dogs or joggers, stand for examination, drop on command when running free, remain under control when in close proximity to cattle, behave in the car, etc. At the moment five dogs have passed this test.

EXPORTS FROM THE UK
As there are so few ACDs in the UK, it is surprising that there have been eight very successful exports to Sweden, Holland and France. Five of these have gone to Sweden. Eugenie Duffourd imported two blue pups, Swordstone Swedish Mist and Swordstone Blue Swede. Swedish Mist quickly became a Swedish, Norwegian and Obedience Champion. Eugenie later imported three Formakin pups by Formakin Kulta out of Baiamul Blue Dinkydi. Annette Vikstrom soon made Formakin Bahloo up to be a Swedish Champion and worked him successfully in Trials.

A young bitch, Kapia Blue Gin (Swordstone Lenthel – Formakin Yindi) went to France to work sheep and cattle. Formakin Boomer (Pwca Blue Boomerang – Aust. Ch. Landmaster Darling Red) went to Holland where he became a Dutch Champion and also obtained the title of Dutch Agility Champion.

SHOW STATUS
In the UK, ACDs were soon making their presence known in Any Variety Not Separately Classified classes at Championship shows. To date, the breed does not have Championship status in the UK. Unlike many other countries, where a dog can become a Champion by winning a certain number of points at designated shows, in the UK a dog must win three Challenge Certificates under three different judges (providing one CC is won after the age of twelve months) in order to become a Champion. The Kennel Club awards CCs at its own discretion. Any breed society may apply to the KC for CCs, but these will not be granted until the KC considers that there are sufficient entries at Open Shows to warrant this. In 1993 ACDs do not yet have sufficient entries.

LEADING SHOW DOGS
For several years ACDs had to compete in AVNSC, but in 1985 the Devon County Open Show put on classes for the breed for the first time in UK, with an entry of fourteen dogs. Our own Formakin Kulta won Best of Breed. In 1986 the National Working Breeds Championship Show gave us our own classes, and twenty-two dogs were entered, with Rose Fisher's Swordstone Ginny (Lenthel Flinton – Lenthel Darlot) taking Best of Breed. Soon several Open and Championship Shows were putting on classes, and Crufts held ACD classes for the first time at the Centenary Show in 1991. John, who judged, made David Hold's Blue Inxs at Rafaell (Drenoss Red Wyola – Tichwell Blue Ribbons) Best of Breed.

Litter Brother and sister Formakin Kulta and Formakin Brolga 1982. Best Opposite Sex and Best AVNSC Crufts 1986 (232 entries).

Sally Anne Thompson.

With so few dogs in the UK, it has been difficult to establish strains. Of those who have tried, the two that have probably made the most impact are our own Formakins and Ros Cartwright's Drenoss ACDs. We were lucky (in fact, the breed was lucky) that Aust. Ch. Landmaster Darling Red was such an outstanding brood bitch. She was the first ACD to be placed at Crufts, the first to win the AVNSC at a Championship Show, and the first to win the Rare Breed Classes at a Championship Show. In three litters she produced ten Championship show winners (including the Dutch Ch. Formakin Boomer), Best of Breed and Crufts winners, and successful Obedience and Working Trial offspring.

Her son, Formakin Kulta, by Pwca Blue Boomerang, had a number of wins to his credit including Best Opposite Sex AVNSC at Crufts in 1986 under Joe Braddon, with his litter sister, Phillipa Castle's Formakin Brolga, beating him for Best of Breed (232 entries). Another win was Best of Breed AVNSC at the big LKA Championship Show in 1988, after which we decided to

Formakin Kimba at Drenoss 1982 (Pwca Blue Boomerang – Aust. Ch. Landmaster Darling Red) Best Bitch ACD Society of GB Open Show, 1988, and foundation bitch for the Drenoss kennel. Owned by R. Cartwright.

Hartley.

Drenoss Red Wyola 1985 (Slipwood Yippee Formakin Kimba at Drenoss): Consistent winner in the UK, and Best of Breed Crufts 1992. Bred and owned by R. Cartwright.

Hartley.

retire from showing. Another son, G. Lcatt's Formakin Kapira of Ischol, went Best of Breed at the ACD Society of GB Open Show in 1988.

Ros Cartwright founded her strain with the red bitch Formakin Kimba (from the same litter as Formakin Kulta etc.). Mated to Sonia Wright's Slipwood Yipee (Formakin Digger – Swordstone Rozella) Kimba produce a good litter which included the two outstanding dogs, Drenoss Red Wyola and Drenoss Red Impudence. Ros kept Wyola who, amongst many other wins, was Best in Show at the Society's first Open Show in 1987 (with Bill Weston judging) – a success he repeated in 1989. In 1992 Wyola was Best of Breed at Crufts, with Ferelith Somerfield judging. At the

Drenoss Red Impudence (brother to Wyola): A multiple Best of Breed and AVNSC winner.

Lindsay.

same show Drenoss Follow Me (Drenoss Foster – Formakin Kimba at Drenoss) was Best Opposite Sex. In 1993 Best of Breed went to Mrs W. E. Nicholls-Miller's Morrow Blue Attunga (Warrigal Blue Todd at Chippinghay – Boomerang Blue Alberta at Morrow), and Best Opposite Sex went to Stella Smyth's Boomerang Blue Alberta at Morrow (Can. Ch. Bluepine Rebels Rip – Yambungan Bunyip).

Drenoss Red Impudence went to Colin Smith, who has probably done more than anyone to show the breed to the public by consistently and successfully campaigning 'Red' all over the country. Red has won the Society's Lismear Shield (for show points won throughout the year) four times. He also won Best of Breed AVNSC at the LKA in 1989, and has had innumerable other good wins.

The Earl and Countess of Huntingdon have done well with their imported bitch, Rokeglen Blue Mankara, who has twice been Best in Show at the ACD Society Open Show. She is also the dam of Monica Gibbon's Warrigal Blue Todd at Chippinghey (Kapia Red Gum – Rokeglen Blue Mankara), the Best Opposite Sex winner at the ACD Society Open Show in 1991.

There are now more shows putting on breed classes, and more judges who seem to know the Breed Standard. Although numbers are still small, there is great enthusiasm amongst exhibitors and breeders, which augurs well for the future.

WORKING DOGS

There has been a lot of interest in ACDs from Obedience and Working Trial enthusiasts, but to get anywhere in these sports you need a lot of dedication. One person who has this in abundance is Stella Smyth, the secretary of the ACD Society. Stella was the first person to get a Working Trial qualification with an ACD. This was with Ischol Rouseabout Blue at Morrow (Formakin Kapira – Swordstone Rascal). 'Broula' then went on to win his CDX, UDX, and WD qualifications – quite an achievement.

Ishcol Rouseabout Blue at Morrow CDX, UDX, WD (Formakin Kapira – Swordstone Rascal): The first ACD to gain a Working Trials title in the UK. Tracy Morgan.

Not satisfied with this, Stella qualified her imported bitch, Boomerang Blue Alberta at Morrow CD; and, more recently, her Bryblue Diamond (Ravenswing Flint – Swordstone Coral) has qualified CDX, UDX, WD. Another Society member to do well in trials is Monica Gibbons. The first dog she qualified was Formakin Chintoo at Chippinghey (Pwca Blue Boomerang – Aust. Ch. Landmaster Darling Red), who won his CD title. She then qualified Kapia Blue Belah (Lenthel Flinton – Formakin Yindi) CDX.

In Obedience, Carol Snell with Formakin Yindi, and Sonia Wright with Swordstone Rozella, have both had some success. A few dogs have competed in Agility competitions, including Michelle Morris with Lismear Bristol Fashion. Recently there have been several more people who are taking an active interest in this type of competition.

ACDs are very active dogs, and most are keen to have a go at anything that will keep them busy. The dogs mentioned have created a lot of interest in the working potential of the breed, and we hope to see more people competing in the future. There are a few ACDs working on farms in the UK, but there are no trials for them. One did go to a well-known sheepdog trainer in Wales, who found him, not surprisingly, very good with cattle – but not so good as his Border Collies with sheep!

GERMANY

There do not appear to be any great number of ACDs in Germany at present. At the beginning of 1992 there were forty-one ACDs registered. Dr Beatrix Sommer-Locher of the von der Weide am Main prefix, imported her first bitch, Flocki 1, from Canada in 1982, and has since imported more stock. Frau Afra Hasper also imported Yambungan Bunnyip Blue in whelp to Canadian Ch. Bluepine Rebels Rip, and bred two litters from her. After this she gave up ACDs as she found little sale for the puppies.

A bitch from the first litter, Boomerang Blue Alberta was imported to the UK in 1987 by Stella Smyth, and has since qualified CD Ex and UD Ex. Dr Sommer-Locher has bred several litters, but shows very little, being more interested in the working side of her dogs. The sire of one litter was Ligras Blue Camino, who works as a protection dog in Denmark. Camino is owned by S. Lund Pedersen, and was bred by Eugenie Duffourd of the well-known Ligras kennels in Sweden. Two or three dogs of the von der Weide am Main breeding have been exported to Switzerland in recent years, one working as a rescue dog.

In Germany the ACD needs to pass a Working Test before becoming a Champion, but as two of the bitches imported from Canada by Dr Sommer-Locher do not have full three-generation pedigrees, they are not accepted by the VDH (Verband fur das Deutsch Hundewesen). So most German ACDs, at present, cannot become Champions. Agility was officially recognised in

Flocki Von der Weide am Main, backpacking in Germany.   *Karin Schmidt.*

Germany in 1991, and some ACDs are now beginning to compete. There are also official Endurance Trials, and several ACD owners hope to compete with their dogs in the future. Some dogs have started rescue work in Germany, and others are at work on farms.

SOUTH AFRICA

The ACD has been recognised in South Africa since 1963, but is still a numerically small breed with no breed society. The Breed Standard used for judging is the one used by the English Kennel Club. The average number of registrations for the past ten years was twenty-two, there being twenty in the year 1990/91. Probably because of the small number shown, and the large area covered by the Kennel Union of South Africa, there has not yet been a South African Champion.

A German ACD retrieving over a six-foot obstacle.   Claudia Schmidt.

KENYA

The first imports into Kenya were in 1950, with a total of ten imports between 1950 and 1989, all being shared between three or four people. A total of ninety-six puppies had been registered by 1989, since when there have been no registrations. The first two imports were Talangab Brutus, a dog from Western Australia which was later made up to Champion, and a bitch, Kalamunda Peach from Victoria.

In 1974 Millflow Captain (half-brother to the famous Aust. Ch. Millflow Ross, who was exported to USA) arrived, and then came Trueheel Blue Buckaroo from Victoria. It is interesting that a blue bitch, Olechuga Blue Maralinga, by Buckaroo out of a bitch by Millflow Captain, was imported into the UK in 1981 by Julie Horne.

At the time of writing, there is only one Champion in Kenya, Curio Blue Baron, owned by Mrs J. R. Chana. To become a Champion, a dog must win three CCs under three different judges. As there are only three shows a year in which ACDs can take part, it can take a very long time to make up a Champion. We have been told that there are a number of ACDs working on cattle ranches in Kenya, but probably most of these are unregistered.

SWEDEN

Sweden, like the other Scandinavian countries, is very keen on Working dogs working. All dogs have to pass a Character Test before becoming Champions. In this, they have to do Obedience, face unusual objects and persons, ignore gunfire, and so on. There is a more difficult test called Korning – or, as the Swedes say, the dog is 'Korad'. Before taking this test, the dog must be at least twenty-two months old, and not past the age of four years. The dog must also have been tested free of HD, been tattooed, and have gained a first prize under a special judge.

All pups have to be registered before being sold, and examined by a vet, who issues a description and health information, including any defects he finds. Teeth are an important point, as they are in most European countries, a full mouth and a correct bite being essential.

Nordic Ch. and Obedience Ch. Blueys Josephine (Sw. Ch. Wooleston Jungle Jon – Sw. Ch. Stormkappans Jessica): the first ACD owned by Eugenie Duffourd in 1978.

Nordic Ch. and Obedience Ch. Swordstone Swedish Mist (Lenthel Flinton – Lenthel Darlot) with puppies by Sw. Ch. Wooleston Jungle Jon. Owned by Eugenie Duffourd.

Circle Red Atherton (Landmaster Showdon – Ligras Blue Piccadilly), bred by Eugenie Duffourd.

Galwarri Kombina, imported by Eugenie Duffourd.

The first Australian import was in 1973 when the Stormkappans kennel imported Wooleston Blue Jumbuc, followed in 1974 by the bitch Wooleston Blue Julie. In 1976 and 1980 the Monstigens Kennel also imported two dogs from Australia, Wooleston Jungle Jon and Landmaster Kemberlee. Next, Eugenie Duffourd of the Ligras kennel imported a dog and bitch from the UK – Swordstone Blue Swede and Swordstone Swedish Mist. Soon after that a dog came in from Norway, and several more from Australia. In 1987 the Ligras kennel again imported from the UK, this time a blue bitch, Formakin Rari. At the same time, another dog and bitch from the same litter went to Sweden. More recently other imports have arrived from Australia.

Nearly all the above mentioned imports have succeeded in obtaining their Swedish Championships, and several have obtained working qualifications. Wooleston Jungle Jon passed a test working with sheep; Swordstone Blue Swede was the International Nordic Winner in 1985, and Swordstone Swedish Mist became a Swedish and Norwegian Champion, and also passed in Tracking and the Korning test. A Swedish-bred dog, Ligras Blue Kamino, already a Dutch and Danish Champion and holder of the German title Bundesieger, was World Winner at the World Show, held in Copenhagen in 1989.

A large number of ACD pups are sold to farmers in Sweden and prove very successful working stock. Many farmers say they prefer them to the Border Collies and other dogs they have tried, as the ACD is a much tougher worker, and works instinctively. Stock has been exported to other European countries for showing and working, some going to Switzerland to be trained for Search and Rescue. The ACD in Sweden is therefore in a healthy state, with a number of dogs being able to use their potential for work in various spheres.

FINLAND
In 1992 there were approximately two hundred ACDs registered with the Finnish Kennel Club. There is a flourishing ACD Society, with a good membership. The first import was in 1984, and that was Ligras Blue Connie from Eugenie Duffourd's kennel in Sweden. Since then, several more have been imported from the Ligras kennels, including Ch. Ligras Kim Orange Boy, owned by Marja Vornanen. This dog was Best Puppy and Best Red Male in 1991; European Winner in 1991 and '92. He is also a working dog, competing in Tracking competitions.

In 1987 Stockmate Blue Charm and Ratuman Blue Sheila arrived from Australia. There were three more Australian imports in 1991, and another in 1992. Also in 1992, a red bitch was

Fin. Ch. Ligras Kim Orange Boy 1990. European Junior Winner, Winner 1992. Best Red Male in Finland in 1991 and 1992. Owned by Marja Vornanen.

Fin. Ch. Cranefield's Blue Xmasstar, competes in the show ring, in Obedience, and also does rescue work. Owned by Mari Jormanainen.

Pia Makinen.

Fin. and Int. Ch. Cranefield's Hereford Red 1987 (Ligras Red Dompierre – Ligras Blue Connie). Owned by Kauko Seppanen and Matti Kariniemi.

Fin. Ch. Cranefield's Jungle Jolka 1989, a Show and Obedience winner. Owned by Paivi Uttuslien and Harri Viirumaki.

imported from the Reddenblue Kennels of Canada. So it can be seen that the breed is obviously in a very healthy state with such a variety of bloodlines. Another well-known winner is Mari Jormanainen's Ch. Cranefields Blue Xmasstar. He has also won well in Rescue Competitions and Obedience, and sometimes works with the Finnish Red Cross and the Police. Apparently, he also works cattle, once again proving the versatility of the breed.

Luckily for the ACD population, the Finns appear to be very keen on working competitions, of which there are five: Tracking, Search (a purely Scandinavian event), Message Dog, General Class, and Protection Dog. The latter is run under IPO – International Prufung Order – rules. Each competition has Novice, Open and Championship classes; dogs have to pass in the lower classes before moving up.

To become a Finnish Champion, a dog must first gain three certificates, one when it is at least two years old. The dog must also pass a Character Test, or obtain a pass in a Working Competition.

Pavesi Blue Justin 1991 (Pavesi Blue Jenerra – Pavesi Blue Joesi). Bred by Ella Park, Australia, owned by Tuulia Kauppinen.   *Karin Schmidt.*

There would appear to be little chance of the show ACDs losing their working ability, as most of the dogs work cattle. There are also Herding Trials with both cattle and sheep. Other activities popular with owners and dogs are Agility and Rescue work.

HOLLAND

ACDs first arrived in Holland in the seventies when J. M. van Ommen Kloeke-Evers imported a dog and bitch, Edgiree Happy Jackeroo and Wooleston Blue Cammile from Australia. These two blues quickly became Dutch Champions, and together they produced many litters, one being the blue dog, Pwca Blue Boomerang, exported to the UK in 1980.

During the eighties Roydale Blue Vibrant, Roydale Blue Waltz and Gembecca Little Peggy all came in from Australia. In 1984 Formakin Boomer (Pwca Blue Boomerang – Aust. Ch. Landmaster Darling Red) was imported from the UK. Boomer soon became a Dutch Champion, and in 1988 was Dutch Agility Champion. During his time in Holland, he has also sired numerous winners. In 1992 there were approximately sixty registered ACDs in the country, and several unregistered ones.

The Dutch ACD, Ann Houdijk's Boomerang Blue Alaska (born in Germany), was World Champion Bitch at Dortmund in 1991. Luxemburg Ch. Damaran Dingas Zoe, bred by Arie Witte, was World Champion bitch at Barcelona in 1992. On the working side, Damaran Yindi's Ping-Pong has recently been exported to Switzerland to be trained for Search and Rescue work.

The Dutch are keen on Agility and other dog sports. In 1991 Arie and Anneke Witte organised an ACD event at Assen. There was a large gathering of ACD enthusiasts with over one hundred people and forty dogs. The dogs were all assessed by Mia Van Ommen Kloeke, who gave a running commentary on each one. This was written down and handed to the owners. After the conformation assessment, there were Obedience demonstrations, Agility and Flyball, followed by videos of ACDs. As this proved so popular it is hoped to organise similar events in the near future. This will give the many Dutch people who are interested in the breed a chance to see a number of them together, where they can study the conformation of the dogs and also see them in action.

Dutch Ch. Formakin Boomer competing in Agility.

Damaran Yindi, Arie Witte's Dutch Show and Obedience winner. Claudia Schmidt.

NEW ZEALAND

Although New Zealand is a near neighbour of Australia, the ACD does not seem to be as popular there as in its native country. Since the New Zealand Kennel Club started keeping computer records in 1979, there have been 740 ACDs registered. Obviously, not all these are still living.

To become a Champion in New Zealand, a dog must win eight Challenge Certificates under at least five different judges, which makes it quite difficult for a dog to obtain this title. Like Australia, New Zealand does not have any specific Cattle Dog Trials for the breed, but occasionally ACDs are entered in the trials run by the NZ Sheepdog Trial Association.

Although the number of ACDs actually shown is not very great, there are probably quite a large number of unregistered dogs working on farms in New Zealand.

Chapter Six

CHOOSING THE RIGHT DOG

There always have been, and always will be, advantages and disadvantages in owning a dog. It is a bit like marriage: you hope that the former will outweigh the latter – sometimes they do and sometimes they don't! What we shall try to discuss are the pros and cons of the ACD in comparison to other breeds. As we have already said, the breed is different from any other breed we have known.

BREED CHARACTERISTICS
The ACD is a normal dog, evolved to do a job of work. As a result the breed is relatively free from abnormalities such as hip dysplasia, with which so many other breeds are afflicted. The only serious hereditary problem would seem to be deafness, which we shall be dealing with a little later on. The breed is a handy size for most people – neither a big dog nor a small one. But the ACD has quite extraordinary strength and courage. We have seen one thrown four feet in the air by a kick from a steer, land on his feet and go straight back in to teach the steer a lesson. While this strength was necessary for the work the ACD was bred to do, it is not always an asset when the dog is kept as a companion. It needs a strong man to take an ACD for a walk if the dog has learned to pull on the lead, instead of being taught to walk properly to heel.

We have already referred to the breed's propensity to stay with the owner. Those who have owned a dog who disappears over the horizon to come back in an hour, or perhaps tomorrow, will realise what an enormous asset that is. A walk in the country can be a relaxing and enjoyable experience, instead of a tense and worrying one. The ACD is a great swimmer. In Australia it was reported that an owner left his dog at home when he went sailing. The dog escaped and swam three miles out to sea to join his master. That is just the sort of thing we would expect one of the breed to do.

VERSATILITY
Apart from being strong, the breed is extremely athletic. Considering the average size, the ACD is an exceptional jumper and capable of easily negotiating all the standard obstacles found in Working and Obedience Trials in the UK, USA, and most other countries. The vast majority enjoy Agility, Fly-ball, and any other activity calling for athleticism and enthusiasm, including shutzhund training. The ACD has a good nose and has been successfully trained for the detection of drugs and explosives. In several European countries, ACDs are working as Search and Rescue Dogs.

Ch. Wagga Wagga Blue Ace is working in California as a qualified Police Dog or "K9 Cop" and

*Marja Vornanen's
Fin. Ch. Ligras
Orange Boy and
Cranefield's
Parakoola Dingo.
The ACD is a handy
size, neither big nor
small, but the breed
possesses
extraordinary
courage and
strength.*

Pia Makinen.

is apparently a great success. This seems to have surprised some people, but there is no reason why the ACD, with its exceptional strength and courage, should not hold its own with any of the generally accepted police dog breeds. However, care would have to be taken not to use those that were naturally aggressive. Ace would appear to have a very stable temperament, and his training hasn't changed his friendly attitude towards friendly people.

When someone asks if a breed is good with children, we usually ask if the children are good with dogs! In fact, the ACD really is good with children and becomes very attached to them. The breed also has a very strong guarding instinct, which can be an asset or a liability, according to prevailing circumstances. An old-fashioned parent who decides that his child would benefit from a good smack, may find that the dog disagrees!

AGGRESSION

The breed is supposed to be suspicious of strangers, but a dog should not be aggressive towards them. Unfortunately, some are, and care should be taken to avoid one that is over-aggressive. Aggression towards people is quite unconnected with aggression towards other dogs. Dogs which fight for the hell of it – as opposed to those that fight through fear – are usually very amiable with children and quite often with puppies too.

Our observations suggest that ACDs in Canada and the US are much less aggressive than those in the UK and Australia. This could be due partly to breeding, and partly to upbringing, or probably a combination of both. Some people we met in the US were worried about the lack of "fire" in some American dogs, and they were afraid that it might lead to a lack of working ability. However, there is not much likelihood of this happening, for a dog's instinct to fight has absolutely no connection with the instinct to herd or heel cattle.

Roydale Blue Vibrant and her daughter, Damaran Yindi. The ACD is an extremely athletic dog.

Flecki Von der Weide am Main 1991 (Boomerang Blue Amos – Dorlev d Weide am Main): training for Search and Rescue work in Switzerland.

INTELLIGENCE

Of course, the ACD is intelligent, as are the vast majority of breeds. But intelligence does not make a dog trainable. In fact, intelligence can, and frequently does, make a dog quite untrainable. It depends on whether the dog uses intelligence to understand the wishes of the owner, or whether a dog uses that intelligence to find ways of evading those wishes. A stupid dog is less likely to take advantage of a stupid owner than an intelligent one. What is wanted is a dog that is amenable to training – and that certainly applies to the ACD.

TRAINING

Not surprisingly, a highly intelligent and versatile dog that was originally bred to work and to keep on working, is not going to think much of sitting in a flat all day while the owner goes to work. Unless the owner provides an outlet for the ACD's physical and mental energy, the dog will almost certainly find one – and this can, and frequently does, lead to all sorts of trouble.

All dogs should be trained in elementary Obedience, to come when called, to lie down and stay there, and to walk on a slack lead. The ACD *must* be trained. A trained dog is likely to provide enormous pleasure; an untrained dog will provide endless worry and anxiety. Before deciding to have an ACD it is very important that you decide whether you are capable of, and willing, to provide the facilities which this very special dog requires and deserves. If your answer to that is in the affirmative, the next task is to find the right dog. We are often asked what is the most important factor in training, and our answer is always the same – finding the right dog to train for that owner's particular purpose.

INHERITANCE VERSUS ENVIRONMENT

What we have just been saying about the breed is a generalisation. The characteristics we have described apply to the majority of ACDs. However, it is the minority which do not answer this description that cause trouble and disappointment, and great care should be taken to avoid them.

Every puppy is born with certain inherited characteristics. The adult dog depends on how these characteristics are affected by the environment. It is rather like building a house. Two builders using exactly the same materials can end up with two very different houses. A good builder can make quite a good job with inferior material, and a bad builder can make a pretty awful mess with the very best material. However, the best houses are built by good builders using the very best materials.

Likewise with dogs. Some people can start with a very mediocre puppy and end up with quite a good dog, while others can take a very promising puppy and completely ruin it. The best dogs are those with good breeding, reared and trained by people who make the best use of their inherent potential. We believe that the ultimate dog depends fifty per cent on inherited characteristics and fifty per cent on how these characteristics are developed. There are those who disagree, including some for whom we have the greatest respect; but we have found no evidence to make us change our minds.

THE PEDIGREE

The best guide to how a puppy will grow up mentally and physically must therefore be in the pedigree. To most people a pedigree is a piece of paper with a lot of names on it, often with the names of Champions underlined or in red ink. To an expert on the breed it is a picture of a lot of dogs, which he knows either personally or by repute.

Some people, including some who should know better, believe that if a name appears more than once in a pedigree the dog is in-bred and will almost certainly be subject to all sorts of weaknesses. In-breeding produces nothing – it only accentuates what is already there. If a mother and son, or father and daughter are mated, the progeny are likely to inherit the characteristics of the dam/grandam or sire/grandsire good *or* bad. The danger of breeding as close as this is in case some unknown weakness makes an appearance. However, it is important to bear in mind that all our breeds of pedigree livestock, including the ACD, have been produced by very close in-breeding.

All wild species are in-bred to some extent, often very closely for many generations. The reason they have survived, and sometimes multiplied to plague proportions, is because of one of the oldest rules of nature – survival of the fittest. Dog breeders of old believed in that rule. As Kaleski says of the Bagust brothers: "They bred a lot and drowned a lot." It would be highly unlikely if they would even have considered hand-rearing a puppy which refused to suck, or if the dam had insufficient milk.

The characteristics which you should look for in the ancestry of a puppy depend, to a great extent, on the purpose for which you want a dog. If you eventually hope to show the dog, the Champions in the pedigree will be of considerable importance. If, on the other hand, you want a dog solely as a companion, they are of no importance at all – except, perhaps, to brag to your friends about the prizes your dog's grandfather won in the show ring! The same applies if you want a dog to work cattle. There is, of course, no reason why the same dog should not answer all three purposes. Such a dog may be a little more difficult to find, but there are many dogs, particularly in Canada and the US, who prove that it can be done.

BAD TEMPERAMENT

No matter what you want your dog to do, the one characteristic which should be avoided at all costs is nervousness, usually referred to as bad temperament. This occurs in all breeds and has nothing to do with in-breeding. It can be attributed to two distinct causes.

Firstly, it is the result of a natural tendency to return to nature. A lot of domestic rabbits of many different breeds end up looking like wild rabbits if left to breed indiscriminately. It is now generally acknowledged that all domestic dogs are descended from the wolf, whose existence depended on the survival of the fittest. But it also depended on its ability to evade its enemies, the most dangerous of all being man. As with the Dingo, a friendly wolf would very soon become a dead wolf; while the shy, furtive animal would live to propagate the species. Strangely enough, both wolves and Dingoes kept in captivity often become very friendly and affectionate towards humans – but by no means all.

The second reason for the prevalence of nervousness in all breeds of domestic dogs, in some breeds more so than others, is not in-breeding itself, but in-breeding from nervous stock. If the same name frequently recurs in a pedigree, it is important to make quite sure that the particular animal has a bold, steady temperament. If this individual is at all nervous, it is almost certain that some of the progeny, probably most of the progeny, will be nervous. The totally unnatural conditions under which the vast majority of dogs are forced to live today makes it more and more important to pick a puppy with a good temperament.

As we said earlier, no two dogs are identical, even those from the same litter, and neither are any two dog owners. A dog that is a complete failure with one owner can, and quite often does, become a great success with someone else. What you want is a dog to suit *you*, not forgetting that you are only buying fifty per cent of the finished article. The other fifty per cent depends on how you bring up the puppy. Some people claim as much as eighty per cent for upbringing, but one thing is certain: rearing a puppy with a good temperament is far more enjoyable than rearing one with temperamental weaknesses, and you will end up with a better dog too.

THE IMMEDIATE FAMILY

Few prospective dog owners understand pedigrees, and it is not always easy to get advice from someone who does. It is usually possible, however, to find out quite a lot about the immediate relatives. On no account should anyone buy a puppy without seeing the dam, who influences the puppy more than the sire.

The late Derek Freeman, a very good friend, who was Breeding Manager of the Guide Dogs For The Blind Association for thirty years, carried out an experiment with two Labrador bitches that whelped at the same time. Bitch 'A' was gun-shy, and bitch 'B' was not. He divided the litters, which were by the same sire, putting half the 'B' puppies with bitch 'A', and vice versa. All the puppies reared by the gun-shy bitch were gun-shy; while none of the puppies on bitch 'B' were afraid of bangs. That was only one experiment, but it is highly significant. The influence of the dam is noticeable in other species too. Generally speaking, friendly mares have friendly foals. More noticeable for those who have to cope with the progeny of mares which are bad to catch – they nearly all seem to be even worse than their mothers!

The sire, of course, is important too. He may not be owned by the breeder. In which case, it is worth making an effort to see him either at home, or at a show, or some other convenient place. If the sire and the dam are not the sort of dog you would like to own, *do not buy a pup from the litter.* It may be possible to see some other relatives – grand-dams, brothers, sisters and cousins etc. Make sure you have a chance to handle them, and do not pay any attention if you are told that ACDs are supposed to be suspicious of strangers.

A dog that refuses to be handled by anyone, even when in the company of the owner/pack leader, is either nervous or over-aggressive. Such a dog may be both nervous *and* aggressive, in which case this is potentially a very dangerous animal. There is no need for a dog to show any liking for a stranger, or even to tolerate being mauled about by one of those 'dog lovers' who put their face right up to the dog's nose! All that is needed, is for you to stroke and handle the ACD, without the dog attempting to escape or to bite.

Many bitches are very protective towards their puppies, which is quite natural and excusable. But by the time the pups are six weeks old, some of the protective instinct has usually worn off. In any case, it is her offspring she should be protecting; if she is removed from them she should be "amenable to handling", as required by the Breed Standard.

If you want a dog to work – and hopefully some of you will – look for a pup bred from working stock. There are few ACDs that have no working instinct, even those bred from stock which has not worked for several generations. Given the opportunity, an eight-week-old pup is quite likely to nip the heel of a cow, but that is no indication as to *how* the dog will work. If you want a good worker, try to find a puppy bred from a strain of good workers.

Assuming that you have found a litter and that you like the breeding, the next task is to pick the best puppy for yourself, and it is worth going to a great deal of trouble in making your choice. Hopefully, your dog is going to be with you for a long time, even longer than you may expect. The oldest dog in the *Guinness Book of Records* is an ACD in Australia who lived to be twenty-nine, and was still working cattle at well over twenty!

MALE OR FEMALE

Some people have difficulty deciding whether to have a dog or a bitch. Size could be of some relevance in deciding. As in all normal breeds, as opposed to those that have been 'improved' for the show ring, the male ACD is appreciably larger than the female. A seventeen inch bitch is really quite a lot smaller than a twenty-two inch dog.

THE CASE FOR NEUTERING

Unless we want to breed from a dog or a bitch, we have the animal neutered, and have done so for many years with no regrets. Many dogs spend a lifetime of almost continual frustration with bitches in season quite near, but still out of reach. We have found that any changes in character resulting from castration are changes for the better. Because dogs are usually castrated when quite young, few people have the opportunity to compare an animal before and after the operation.

We have had many dogs castrated at up to six years of age – our own and others in our care – and have never found any change in the guarding instinct or working ability. A castrated dog is less likely to be aggressive to other dogs, less likely to leave his 'trade mark' on your neighbour's gate post, or worse still, the furniture if you are asked in. Nor will he go off after your neighbour's bitch when she comes in season. Having fewer affairs of his own to attend to, he is more likely to concentrate on your affairs, which will make him much easier to train.

Castration should not be regarded as a cure for all evils. A dog which has developed a liking for fighting is almost certain to still want to fight, especially if his old rivals are around. A nervous dog will still be nervous. Speaking generally, a castrated dog is usually much less trouble to his owner and much happier himself than if he were entire.

Spaying a bitch is usually done for the benefit of the owner, but it can be just as beneficial to the bitch. She will not have to be kept shut up for three weeks when she comes in season twice a year. This can be a very traumatic experience for some bitches, and can have a lasting effect. A spayed bitch does not have false pregnancies, which is usually another stressful time, and she will not develop pyometra or other uterine problems later in life.

One of the best vets we ever had (now retired) kept a record of all bitches which attended her surgery. This showed conclusively that spayed bitches required much less veterinary care than those that were not spayed. She advised breeders to have their brood bitches spayed when they were no longer required for breeding. For those who did not want to breed, she advised spaying at a much earlier age.

Some people claim that obesity will result from neutering. Many entire animals of both sexes are obese, for the same reasons that people are overweight – too much food and too little exercise! Guide Dogs for the Blind are all neutered, and it is very unusual to see one that is too fat. The only disadvantage we have found as a result of neutering is a profuse coat; some types of coat seem to be affected more than others. We have only seen one ACD which was affected, but there may be others.

THE AGE TO NEUTER

There is an enormous difference of opinion as to the best age at which either dogs or bitches should be neutered, and these opinions seem to keep changing. Some vets will castrate puppies at eight weeks old, or even less. An American veterinarian we spoke to subscribed to this view. His argument was that it had been scientifically proved that the level of testosterone in an adult dog is the same whether he was castrated at eight weeks or eight months. That is probably correct, but we have seen dogs which were castrated as puppies which had never matured, either mentally or physically. They were canine eunuchs and certainly not the sort of dog we would want to own.

Guide Dogs for the Blind are all castrated, and it has been found that the age at which this is done is very important. Castrated too late the dog may have developed the habit of lifting his leg, and an interest in lamp posts is not likely to help a blind person! If castrated too early, it was found that the dog is likely to lack the initiative necessary to lead a blind person. Vets like to castrate early, because it is a simpler operation. It should be remembered that a lot of owners cannot cope with a dog that shows much initiative.

Leg raising is the most obvious sign that a young dog is reaching maturity. To us, it does not matter if he lifts his leg after castration, so we err on the side of having a dog operated on too late rather than too early. If a youngster shows any sign of being aggressive to other dogs, it is important to have him castrated before he gets into a real fight.

It used to be generally accepted that a bitch should not be spayed until after her first season. There now seems to be some evidence that no harm is done in spaying before then, provided she is a mature puppy. We had one of our bitches spayed before she came into season, but she was nine months old, and was very mature. At the GDBA, it is still the general practice to leave bitches until after their first season before having them spayed. Our frequent references to the GDBA are because we have known many of the personnel there for many years, and the Association has kept records referring to thousands of dogs –probably more than any other organisation.

PICKING A PUPPY

Now for the big decision – choosing the puppy, which you hope will grow into the sort of dog you want. The modern idea is to have the litter assessed by a professional assessor. Starting in the US, this idea is now becoming popular in the UK, and some other countries too. Breeders have the whole litter assessed, and this enables them to offer prospective customers a sort of print-out of each puppy's character.

This is a great idea in theory, but we are yet to be convinced that it works. There are others who share our doubts. The following is quoted from the *Waltham Book of Dog and Cat Behaviour,* 1992:

"It was originally thought that dominance hierarchies were already being established at this stage (under eight weeks) which were retained into adulthood. Studies of wolf cubs have shown this to be the case with dominance at eight weeks of age correlating well with dominance at one year old (Fox 1972). This led to a propensity of "puppy tests" commonly carried out at six to eight weeks of age, attempting to predict fear-related, aggressive, or owner-directed dominance behaviour in later life. In practice, these tests achieved little success (M. S. Young, personal communication).

"In recent years there have been a number of detailed investigations into the development of social behaviour in litters of puppies (Wright 1980, Nightingale 1991, Hoskin 1991). These studies have shown considerable fluidity in dominance hierarchies of litters, with individual puppies moving from the top to the bottom, or the bottom to the top of the hierarchy. In addition, hierarchies measured during social play, or pairwise competitions, tended to produce different results, even when carried out on the same day. From these studies it is becoming clear that social relationships are not fixed until adult life, and that early social tussles can be considered as rehearsals for the roles to be played in later life (Marton 1984)."

We believe that the person in the best position to assess a litter is the breeder. When we expressed this view to someone who assesses puppies, she concurred but added that many breeders are incapable of doing so. Regretfully we have to agree. But whether you want a dog to be a companion, to work, or to show, try to find a breeder who takes a real interest in the individual characters of the puppies. These puppies are likely to have been handled and taken out of their run. This will give them an advantage over puppies whose owner is only interested in the physical qualities.

WHAT AGE TO BUY

At one time few breeders would allow puppies to go to new homes until they were eight weeks old, and it was not considered advisable to start training until the pup was six months old. We used to subscribe to both these theories. However, it is now realised that puppies are affected by their environment at a much earlier age than was previously believed possible. In the early sixties, the GDBA started putting puppies out to 'puppy walking' homes at six weeks of age. They were given a temporary vaccination followed by a full vaccination at twelve weeks.

The idea met with a great deal of scepticism and opposition from the veterinary profession, but thirty years and over 25,000 puppies later, that policy is still being adhered to. The American GDBA has found similar results. If puppies remained at the Guide Dog kennels for over twelve weeks before being homed, then only thirty per cent went on to become Guide dogs; if they were

Formakin puppies aged six weeks. The breeder is in the best position to assess the litter, as he or she should know the individual characters of the puppies.

Sally Anne Thompson.

Puppies are affected by their environment from an early age.

Claudia Schmidt.

homed before twelve weeks then ninety per cent were successful (Pfaffenburger & Scott 1975).

In spite of this evidence, there are still vets who adhere to the old-fashioned course of vaccinations and advise owners to keep the puppy on their own ground until fourteen weeks of age. So the puppy spends the first six to eight weeks in the breeder's kennels, and the next six to eight weeks in the new owner's garden. Then, on the exact day – almost to the exact hour – when the vet said it would be OK, the puppy is dragged out into the big wide world. To make matters worse, by fourteen weeks the second teeth will be pushing up. From then until teething finishes is a very vulnerable time for the temperament of any puppy, even when reasonably brought up. No wonder there are so many nervous dogs around.

When Derek Freeman told us of the success of his policy with Guide Dogs, we adopted it ourselves and have done so now for over twenty-five years. Some behaviourists who have studied puppies believe that they should be left with the dam until seven weeks. The belief is that the puppy will benefit from an extra week's discipline from the mother, and that the week will serve to sort out the pecking order in the pack of siblings. It would then be easier to socialise the puppy with other dogs. That may be true, but if we were buying, we would try to take a puppy at six weeks. This particularly applies to an ACD puppy, which matures much more quickly than puppies of other breeds.

Apart from being handled and socialised up to the age of six to seven weeks, it is very important that a puppy has clean living quarters. Instinct makes a bitch clean up after puppies while they are still in the nest. As they grow older, instinct will make them go out of the nest to relieve themselves – provided they have somewhere to go; puppies reared in cramped conditions, where they have no option to paddling around in their own faeces and urine, which does happen, will have lost the instinct to be clean.

For those looking primarily for a companion, the best bet is often the small breeder, who has one bitch with puppies reared in the kitchen or utility room. If there are children around, so much the better. That type of breeder is likely to know the individual characters of the puppies better than the breeder with a number of bitches. But remember that sensible breeders are just as anxious to find the right owner for each puppy as you are to find the right puppy for yourself. A disappointed buyer does immense damage to the reputation of both the breeder and the breed – a remark which applies whether the client wants a companion, a show dog, or a worker.

WHAT TO LOOK FOR
TEMPERAMENT

An eight-week-old pup should not be suspicious of strangers, and a six-week-old pup even less so. A puppy that appears suspicious is usually afraid of strangers, and is likely to be afraid of many other unusual experiences which will be encountered later in life. Do not be influenced by assurances that the pup will be OK when you get to know each other: this may happen, or it may not! If a puppy runs away as you approach and will not come back, just leave it there!

Many Shepherds we have known simply call to the puppies, and pick the one that reaches them first. That is usually the dominant one, but then, these were dominant men, who liked a dominant dog. John has always liked a dominant dog, although there have been times when he has wished that the dog would show more interest in what he wanted, rather than in pursuing his own canine pursuits. However, these usually became excellent dogs in time. Not everyone likes that sort of dog, and the majority of owners simply cannot cope with them.

Any breeder who does not know the pecking order of a litter of six-week-old pups is either very unobservant or completely lacking in knowledge of canine behaviour, or both. The breeder should

Temperament is all-important when choosing a puppy.   *Claudia Schmidt.*

also know if the puppies are bred from a line of dominant dogs. If so, it is inadvisable to choose a dominant puppy. If, on the other hand, they are bred from a line of very submissive, possibly sensitive dogs (not very likely in this breed) the dominant pup may well be the best choice. Dominance seems to have become a big problem in recent years, and we shall be discussing this when we come to training.

Allow plenty of time when you go to see a litter of puppies. To begin with they will probably all scrabble at the wire of their run. Clap your hands in front of them, and watch their reactions. The bold puppy will want to investigate, but the shy one, especially the noise-shy one, will run away. If the pup is only startled and comes back to investigate, that is fine. But if the pup will not come near or, worse still, runs away, do not bother with that one. Small puppies, like small children, never persist in anything for very long. Soon they will go off to play, when it will be much easier to study both their characters and their physique.

Pick up the puppy you fancy, and hold the pup in your arms. Some puppies will relax and obviously enjoy being cuddled, while others become quite tense. The former is always to be preferred, although it does depend to some extent on how much handling they have had up to this age. Avoid a puppy who really struggles to get away. Then put the puppy down alone, and observe the pup's behaviour. We like an inquisitive puppy that investigates the surroundings, but not one that goes blundering into trouble. That is unlikely to happen with an ACD pup, and it is here that its Dingo ancestry is likely to be revealed.

We have found that an ACD pup rarely goes straight up to a new-found object, something like a piece of rope – it could be a snake – or perhaps a large stone lying on the ground. On spotting the strange object, the pup usually stops dead, but does not run away. Instead the pup walks cautiously round the object, gradually getting closer, until the decision is made that there is nothing to worry about, and the pup goes straight up to investigate. This cautious, investigative behaviour seems to be peculiar to the ACD. Such behaviour might lead some to believe that the puppy was nervous and afraid of strange objects, which is not the case, but it is sometimes difficult to differentiate between suspicion and fear.

The puppy should respond when spoken to, and come up to be petted when someone squats down in a friendly way. Most trainers, including those at the GDBA, believe that puppies which show a natural inclination to retrieve are likely to be more amenable to training later on. So it is worth playing with a bit of old rope or a rag, and when you have got a pup's interest, try tossing the rope away. Do not expect an 'Obedience' retrieve, but the pup should certainly pick it up, and with a bit of coaxing might even bring it back. Beware the little blighter that stalks off and pays no interest to anyone – although this may depend, to some extent, on how much the pup has been handled.

PHYSICAL APPEARANCE

If you have ambitions to show your pup later on, you will need to pay attention to physical as well as mental qualities. Because they mature so quickly, ACD puppies between six and eight weeks look like little dogs, and many of them even have their ears pricked. If not, hold the puppy upside down in your arms when the ears will fall back so that you can see what they will be like when they are erect. The coat will be softer than in the adult, but it should not be fluffy. The colour and markings will all be there, but will be dull and the speckling will not have come through. As the puppy grows older, the red or blue colour, and also the tan markings on the blues, will become much richer.

A bold puppy usually carries the tail up, often well beyond the perpendicular. But that is nothing

Drenoss Follow Me (Drenoss Foster – Formakin Kimba at Drenoss), BOS Crufts 1992. Bred and owned by R. Cartwright.
If you buy an adult, you can see exactly what you are getting.

to worry about, so long as it is not in a tight curl like a Pug. Examine the teeth, which although tiny, should be in the same position in the mouth as in the adult dog; the lower incisors behind, but touching the upper ones. A slightly overshot or undershot mouth sometimes rights itself with maturity, but not very often. Watch how the puppy moves. A well-built ACD puppy strides along as if the dog really intended going somewhere. Taken all over, the ACD puppy should be pretty much a miniature of what the Breed Standard calls for.

BUYING AN ADULT
Some people prefer to start off with an adult dog, which can have both advantages and disadvantages. If you want a dog to work, you can see the ACD working, learn the commands and hope that the dog will work just as well for you. If this is not the case, it will almost certainly be your fault. And it will no doubt cost a lot of money. Alternatively you might be able to buy a young dog, who has started to work but requires training. This dog will cost more than a puppy, but not only will you feel sure that this ACD *will* work, you should also be able to get some idea of *how* this particular dog will work.

If you want a dog as a companion, there can also be advantages in starting out with an adult. The dog should be house trained, and is likely to be past the puppy chewing stage. The biggest advantage is that you can judge the actual dog, rather than what you hope the dog will grow up to be. An adult dog who is fully vaccinated and has, hopefully, had some training, might be a much better bargain than a puppy. Indeed, many adult dogs are offered free 'to a good home'. However, it is very important that you find out exactly why the owner is so anxious to find a new home for the dog.

It is sometimes very difficult to find homes for adult dogs. There is a common belief that, unless acquired as a puppy, a dog will not become attached to the owner. Absolute rubbish! A moment's thought should be enough to make anyone realise that all Service Dogs, Guide Dogs, Hearing Dogs, Dogs for the Disabled, and many others change hands, sometimes more than once. These dogs become quite devoted to their owners and handlers, and develop a rapport which is quite unknown to many pet owners.

The other reason why people shun a dog of, say, four or five years, is because they think that the dog will not live so long. But many puppies do not live beyond four or five years, and it is debatable whether the expectation of life of the average eight-week-old puppy is much greater than that of a four-year-old dog.

Because of the risk of infection, few breeders, including ourselves, will allow a puppy to go on approval. But if we part with an adult dog we insist that, if, for *any* reason, things do not work out, we must have the dog back. A dog that doesn't fit into one home might be quite happy in another.

CONGENITAL DISEASES

The ACD is relatively free from hereditary defects, but this does not mean that the breed is immune. Both hip dysplasia (HD) and progressive retinal atrophy (PRA) have cropped up in the breed and, in common with most other breeds, hip scoring and eye testing of breeding stock is now the general practice. Some countries will only grant import licences to dogs which carry certificates of freedom from both HD and PRA.

These tests have not eradicated the problem, but they have helped to keep it under control. At one time PRA was prevalent in Border Collies. The International Sheepdog Society then passed a rule saying that only puppies from eye-tested parents could be registered. Since then the incidence of blindness in registered Sheepdogs has dropped to the point where it is now quite rare.

The ACD does have one quite serious congenital defect, and this is deafness in varying degrees. Unfortunately, we have had first-hand experience of this. In her first litter Aust. Ch. Landmaster Darling Red had six puppies, and three of them were deaf. That was something of a bombshell, made worse by the fact that we had sold two of the pups without realising there was anything wrong with them. No one in Australia had even hinted that the odd deaf pup might crop up. Mated to a different dog 'Honey' had no more deaf pups, and we now know a lot more about deafness.

In *Barkers and Biters*, Kaleski warns buyers to make sure the dog is not deaf or blind. We have been told on good authority that deaf dogs have won in the show ring in Australia and that at least one was exported to the US. No one in the UK seems to have had a misfortune similar to ours, and we only hear of the occasional deaf puppy, which is not quite the same as saying there have not been any!

It is extremely difficult to detect a deaf puppy in a litter. If they are all lying or playing together and they hear an unusual sound, the deaf puppy will react the same as the others, appearing to have heard. The easiest time to detect a deaf pup is when the litter are all asleep, but lying separately, as they often do on a warm day. If, as you approach, they all react except one, you can be pretty sure that this pup is deaf.

A squeaky toy can be helpful, but the noise must be made when the puppy is not looking at you, otherwise the pup will probably react to your movement. What is even more difficult to detect, either alone or with the others, is the unilaterally deaf pup. If you make an unusual noise while a puppy is looking away from you, most pups will look around to see where the noise has come from. However, if deaf in one ear, the pup will probably react to the sound, but look in several directions before realising where it came from.

Modern technology has made it possible to identify deafness in quite young puppies by means of Brainstern Auditory Evoked Tests (BAER Tests). These detect not only total deafness, but varying degrees and different types of partial deafness. This enables the breeder to have a totally deaf puppy euthanatised before becoming too fond of it; that is certainly the only humane course to take. The dog's most acute senses are smell and hearing. Unlike a deaf person, a dog cannot communicate by reading or writing, and is therefore unable to enjoy the quality of life which every dog deserves. A dog that is unable to hear an approaching child could easily bite when startled – and no blame can be attached to the dog.

Some puppies recorded as partially deaf in a BAER Test, appear to hear quite well. Provided they can hear commands, and the deafness is bilateral, this may not create a big problem. A unilaterally deaf dog cannot tell where the sound comes from. Whether it is wise to keep such a puppy is debatable. It is quite possible that a unilaterally deaf dog could be startled by a child, if asleep with the good ear to the ground. Whatever the degree of deafness, the puppy should always be neutered if kept.

BAER Testing is being carried out quite extensively in North America, where it is recorded that forty-five breeds are liable to congenital deafness. These include Collies, Bull Terriers and Dalmatians, which is probably why it is to be found in the ACD. Test matings are also carried out to try and determine which lines carry the genes for deafness, and some strains are already clear. Breeders are being recommended to have their breeding stock tested. Tests have also been carried out on puppies in the UK, and probably other countries too. It may well be that in the future certificates of freedom from deafness will be as commonplace as those for HD and PRA. It is to be hoped that this would have the same effect on deafness in the ACD as PRA testing had on blindness in the Border Collie.

BAER Tests can be carried out on puppies at any time from the age of five weeks, and there is no upper age limit. The animal is sedated but not anaesthetised, and there are no signs of stress or discomfort during the testing. For further information, contact your veterinary surgeon.

Chapter Seven

PRINCIPLES OF LEARNING

UNDERSTANDING YOUR ACD

Dogs do not understand any words as we know them. It is just as easy to teach a dog to lie down by saying "get up" as by saying "lie down"; or to get a dog to come to you, by saying "go away." Dogs understand sounds. Their hearing is far more acute then ours, and they can differentiate between different sounds much better than we can.

THE ABILITY TO REASON

There is some difference of opinion as to whether a dog can reason. Scientists say they do not, but these scientists usually work under laboratory conditions. Most people who have trained or worked with dogs can give examples where they were quite convinced that a dog displayed reasoning ability. However, it is very difficult to prove that the dog was not reacting to some instinct, or could hear a sound that was inaudible to human ears. We believe that dogs do reason, but only occasionally, and only if the dog is very clever. Most examples of reasoning develop in the mind of the fond owner, who probably believes that "He understands every word I say to him," when, in fact, the dog does not understand any words at all.

There is one thing that is beyond doubt. It is very unwise to assume that your dog reasons, and even more unwise to assume that if the dog does reason, this power will be used to your advantage! All training must be based on the assumption that your dog does not reason.

ASSOCIATION OF IDEAS

Dogs, like all other higher animals, learn by association of ideas. If an animal does something, either accidentally or intentionally, and finds it enjoyable, then the dog is likely to do the same thing again. If the action proves to be unpleasant, then the chances are that the dog will refrain from doing it again.

The human animal is affected by associations of ideas. When travelling along a road, we might come to a spot which perhaps, quite suddenly, reminds us of something that happened years ago. It could be a nasty accident which would bring back unpleasant memories; or it could be something amusing which would bring back pleasant memories. Indeed, it could be anything which is associated with that particular spot.

It could also be a sound, rather than a place, which creates the association. There are many people of our generation who, on hearing a siren which sounds like an air raid warning, are immediately reminded of air raids of fifty years ago.

Most of us have met people who are afraid of dogs because they were bitten by one in childhood, sometimes very early childhood. Very often, it is a specific breed that they associate with the dreadful experience, and all other breeds are OK. It is sometimes hard to sympathise with these people, who are able to reason. However, for the sake of argument, we will assume that the person has been bitten by an ACD, and is afraid of all ACDs. By adding a little common sense to their reasoning ability, it should be obvious that he/she is no more likely to be bitten by an ACD than by any other breed.

The situation is very different for the dog. If a puppy is attacked by a dog, the pup will not reason that this is a one-off event, and therefore the chances of being attacked by other dogs are slim. The puppy is far more likely to be frightened of all dogs, although the bad experience may be associated with a certain breed, or colour of dog. We have known a puppy who was frightened by a black dog, and was subsequently terrified of all black dogs, but not afraid of any other colour.

When frightened, the dog is faced with two options – fight or flight. The young puppy is inclined to flee, or try to flee. But the adult ACD is rarely inclined to run from danger – quite the reverse. Many a dog, who has never shown the slightest signs of aggression to other dogs, can be turned into a fighter as the result of an unprovoked attack. Here again, the association can be breed or colour selective. It is not unknown for a dog to develop a 'hate' for all dogs of a certain breed, while ignoring those of other breeds.

For the purpose of training, we try to create associations of ideas – those which we want – by correction and reward. By correction, we make it unpleasant for the puppy to do what we deem to be unacceptable, even though the puppy favours this course of action. By reward, we make it pleasant for the puppy to do what we want.

First associations are very important to a puppy. It is unfortunate that the first impression is you, the new owner, taking the puppy from mother and littermates to a strange and often bewildering place. So it is of the utmost importance that you make this transition as pleasant as possible. This can be helped very considerably if you make certain preparations *before* you go to collect your puppy.

PREPARATION FOR YOUR NEW PUPPY
THE GARDEN
Firstly, you must make sure that the house and garden are safe. Cattle Dog pups are notoriously good at exploring and finding a way through, over or under most obstacles – it is a way of life for them! So check the garden fence is puppy-proof. If you have too large a garden to fence completely, make sure that a portion of it is really safe.

While considering the garden, it is a good idea to build a 'digging pit' for the pup. All dogs and puppies love to dig, it is a perfectly natural thing for them to do. But it doesn't make for a happy relationship if your ACD rushes into the kitchen, with muddy paws and your prize rose bush – root and all!

To create a suitable pit, dig out a square about 4ft by 3ft, a foot or so deep, and fill it with sand. Introduce your pup to this area, and show that this is *the* place for digging. This is easily done by burying titbits, liver treats, biscuits, balls etc. You should then find it much easier to teach the pup not to go and dig in the flower beds, by going back to the digging pit with the puppy, and giving the command to "dig".

THE HOUSE
If you are about to have a young puppy in your home, you are probably not excessively house-proud – or if you are, maybe you should have second thoughts! Trailing electric wires have an

All pups love to dig – this one grew up to be Can. Ch. Vitips Downright Dusty, a multiple Breed and Group winner. Bred by Violet Tipping.

immediate, and sometimes fatal attraction to an inquisitive pup, so make sure they are all out of reach. Free standing lamps are just asking to be jumped on and knocked over; objets d'art on low coffee tables always prove tempting, and, apart from the fact that you probably cherish them dearly, if the pup swallows one or chews up the fragments, it could well mean a trip to the vet for an operation. Cupboard doors must be kept shut. So must the bathroom door; the ultimate triumph for any pup is to seize the toilet roll and dash round the house with it!

EQUIPMENT
Your ACD will require a collar and lead. These should be strong but light; soft leather or nylon is best. Do not spend a lot of money on the collar, as the pup will very quickly grow out of it and need a larger one. The best type of feeding bowls are the stainless steel type, which are easy to clean and hard-wearing.

Like a child, a pup needs toys to play with. There are a bewildering array of different playthings on the market, but make sure you only buy good-quality, solid rubber toys, or those made of unchewable nylon, such as Nylabone products. Make sure any balls are too large to be swallowed. Vets all too often have cases brought in where a dog has a ball stuck in the throat or somewhere internal. After all your trouble of choosing and buying suitable toys, you will probably find that your ACD's favourites are such things as pieces of knotted rope, cardboard centres from toilet rolls, old cereal packets and children's teddies. (If the latter are chosen, make sure the eyes are safe.)

An important item, from the pup's point of view is a play pen, similar to those sold for children, or a portable crate. A crate has several advantages, not least that it can be used for the rest of the dog's life. Your pup needs a special, private place, to escape from teasing toddlers and from over-zealous dog-loving friends. A dog needs somewhere to rest after meals, or a safe place to have a chew on a bone.

First put newspaper down inside the crate, and then provide a warm bed to go inside it. Do not bother with a proper dog bed at this stage. A cardboard box from the local supermarket will do fine. As the pup grows you can collect larger boxes. For bedding we have found that synthetic fur fabric is definitely better than blankets. It is easy to wash and dry, reflects the body heat, stays dry if the pup should have an accident, and is virtually unchewable – although there is always the odd ACD to disprove that! Put one of your pup's favourite toys in the bed, and before long, the crate will be regarded as 'home'.

You will also find that a crate is a great help with house training. Few pups will dirty their beds, or their immediate surroundings. If you are too busy to keep an eye on your ACD, you will surely look round and find a damp patch – or worse – on the carpet. If you do not catch the puppy 'in the act', there is nothing you can do about it. But if you see your ACD start getting fidgety when in the crate, you can be ready to whisk the puppy outside. In that way, the pup will soon 'ask' to be let out.

Do not get the idea that the crate is for your puppy to live in – far from it. It is only to make life easier for both of you. Your ACD must learn to stay put, if you have to rush to answer the door or the telephone. By using the crate, the puppy is left somewhere secure and safe. Once in the crate, no one will fall over the puppy, tread on its feet, or, worse still, nag and shout when the puppy is doing nothing 'wrong'. When you go out in the car, your ACD can travel in safety inside the crate. If you need to book a stay at boarding kennels, or if hospitalisation at the vet's is ever required, your dog will already be used to staying in a confined space and will suffer far less stress in consequence.

THE VET

Before collecting your ACD, you should locate a good vet, and make an appointment for the pup to have the necessary injections. The puppy should already have been wormed, but you will need advice on further worming treatments.

NAMING

Make sure that you decide on a name *before* you fetch your puppy home. Nothing is more confusing for the pup than to have the family all arguing about what to call him, and all trying different names. Later on, when the pup's character has developed you will, no doubt, give any number of nicknames, just as we do. In time, your dog will answer to them all, but for now, just stick to one name.

ARRIVING HOME

Once everything is ready, you can arrange a convenient time with the breeder to collect your ACD. Take a friend or member of the family along with you to look after the pup in the car. You want to make your ACD's first association with you as pleasant as possible. So do not shut your dog all alone in the boot behind the dog guard.

Make sure you collect your ACD's pedigree, registration certificate, signed transfer, inoculation certificate (if a course has been started), a record of the worming programme, and what medication was used. Last, but certainly not least, you should be provided with a diet sheet, and a supply of food to last for the first few days. If you are buying from a sensible breeder, the pup should already have been on a collar and lead, and maybe even had a short journey in a car. But even so, the young puppy is still having to leave home and family, which is a very traumatic experience.

First, put a collar and lead on your puppy. ACD pups are, or should be, bright and active, and if you have to stop the car in a hurry there will be no risk of the pup jumping out if the 'minder' has hold of the lead. Have plenty of newspapers and old towels handy. If the puppy is sick, which is very likely, you can 'mop up', and the lap the pup is sitting on will still be dry and comfortable. If your pup is sick, do not scold – no dog does this on purpose. Try not to fuss, and just clean up, settle your puppy, and continue the journey.

On arriving home, let your ACD out in the garden for a run and to have a look around. Do not let the family all rush out to see the new arrival. Wait until you take the pup inside, and then ask them to come in quietly and make friends. At this stage everything is new, and the pup does not want to be overwhelmed by masses of strange people. If it is near a feedtime, mix up a feed and put the bowl in the puppy's crate. You want your ACD to look on the crate as a 'den', and if the pup eats the first meal in there, it will create a happy impression. Do not shut the door, just let your puppy eat, and then it is time to go outside again.

When you take your puppy out, you must stay in attendance. This is the time, right at the beginning, to start house training. Use a word to teach your ACD to eliminate. We use 'hurry up', some people use 'get busy'; it does not matter what you use, so long as you always use the same words. The idea is for the pup to associate the sound with the action. Immediately, and it must be immediately, the pup performs, give plenty of praise and a tidbit, such as a liver treat. Let your puppy play around for a while, and then you can both go back inside.

As we have assumed that you will be collecting your puppy at between six to eight weeks of age, you will be feeding four meals a day. Keep to the same feeding times, and use the food you have been given by the breeder for several days. If you want to change the feed, do so gradually, as otherwise you will end up with a puppy with an upset stomach – not a good start for either of you.

THE FIRST NIGHT

The first night is almost sure to be a noisy one. Your pup has been used to going to bed with siblings in familiar surroundings, and is going to feel very lonely. Before putting your puppy to bed, have a game together, and then take the pup out for a last run and hope you tire him out – not very likely! Then harden your heart; make the crate comfortable with bedding in a box and a toy, put out the light, and leave your puppy to it. Most pups will cry, whine or bark for a while, and then go to sleep. Some settle down straightaway – not many – and the odd one will yell and yell, all night long.

If you can stand it, just leave your puppy. Eventually, which may be a long time, the pup will quieten. Do not scold; you are dealing with a little homesick baby. But do not give in and bring the puppy into your bedroom: you will only be laying up trouble for the future – the next night the puppy will be worse; unless you want a full-grown Cattle Dog on your bed for the rest of its life, put your head under the duvet and try to sleep.

HOUSE TRAINING

Get up early the next morning and take your puppy straight out. Do not worry if the newspaper is dirty; few young pups can last through the night at this age. Use whatever command you have decided on for your puppy to eliminate, give lots of praise and offer a tidbit. Have a game with your pup before returning inside. This is important. If you go back in immediately the puppy has urinated, the pup will very soon decide that the best way of staying outside is not to perform when asked. In which case, instead of spending minutes waiting for action, you could be spending hours. But with praise, tidbits and a game, you should be well on the way to getting the message through.

When you get back inside, feed breakfast, and then take your ACD straight out again. The golden rule is to take your puppy out after every meal, after a drink, when the pup wakes up, and when the puppy goes to the door and starts to look uneasy. This is how a puppy can be house trained by reward alone. But although it works with the vast majority of puppies, there is always the occasional exception. A puppy instinctively wants to keep sleeping quarters and the surroundings clean. Instincts, however, vary enormously in strength and may, on occasion be absent altogether. For example, there is the occasional puppy which will not suckle, or the bitch which refuses to allow her pups to suckle. Instincts can also be strengthened or weakened by use, or by lack of use. As mentioned earlier, this instinct is likely to be considerably weakened in puppies reared in cramped, dirty conditions, and it may have died out altogether.

So if you have a puppy, which for some reason, does not respond to reward and simply messes at any time, and in in any place, it will be necessary to combine reward with correction. At one time correction was considered more important than reward – with children as well as dogs! All that has changed in recent years; we fully approve of the more humane attitude to training which has taken place. Indeed, John was one of the first writers to advocate some of the changes, in his book, *The Family Dog*, first published in 1957 and now in its thirteenth edition.

However, when a pendulum changes direction, it is liable to swing too far the other way. Because of all the readily available advice they now receive, owners are often reluctant to apply even mild correction the first time a puppy makes a mistake. As a result, the dog may require very severe correction later on. It is important to remember that you cannot over-reward, but it is very easy to over-correct. It is also very easy to apply correction at the wrong time, which can, and often does have disastrous consequences.

With the puppy that does not respond to house training by reward only, the essential for success is still constant vigilance. Be on constant alert, and as soon as you see signs of squatting, pick up your puppy quickly, at the same time uttering a harsh "No". There is no need to shout; it is the tone of voice that matters, not the volume. Take the puppy out, and if you have been lucky enough to avoid an accident, stay outside and use your command to encourage the puppy to perform. When you get the right response, reward it as before.

Picking the puppy up quickly, is, in itself a correction, which the puppy should associate with what it was doing – or was about to do. Next time the puppy feels uncomfortable, the feeling will be associated with correction, and the pup will begin to look uneasy. The observant owner should notice this and take the pup out, before there is the chance of an accident. Do not forget to reward when your puppy performs. If the puppy makes a mistake again, more severe correction can be applied by giving a shake as you pick the puppy up and uttering a harsher "No". Most pups quickly get the message, and will soon "ask" to go out. Until it becomes a habit, it is a good idea to take the puppy out, encourage it to perform, and then reward.

A common mistake is often made when people go out and leave the puppy shut up. When they return and find a puddle on the floor, they punish the poor little mite, even though the puppy does not understand the 'crime', and couldn't help it anyway. On top of that, the puppy may well have gone to greet the owner, and is met with a punishment. The result is that the puppy quickly becomes afraid of the owner – who usually believes that the puppy is 'looking guilty' – and the situation goes from bad to worse.

Because dogs do not reason, it cannot be explained to them that they have done something wrong. Correction, when it is necessary, should be applied when the dog is actually doing something wrong. It is also effective to correct the dog at the moment a 'crime' is being contemplated, when the dog's mind is focused on the action. An educated dog usually knows quite well when it has done something wrong, but this is not true of a young puppy. Correction after the event will do no good, and will probably do untold harm. So, if you leave your puppy and find a puddle on the floor when you return, blame yourself and mop it up.

ESSENTIALS OF TRAINING
THE RECALL
Why do so many dogs refuse to come when called? Because their owners have taught them not to come – not intentionally, but nevertheless very effectively. There is nothing clever about animals going towards a sound which they associate with reward – usually food. Sheep which are very clever, cattle which are not very clever, and fowls which are downright stupid, will all run to the sound they associate with food. The sound can be a human voice, a whistle, or it may be the sound of the tractor or the rattle of a bucket. It matters not what the sound is, so long as the animal associates it with reward, which means that it must always be the same. Cattle which respond to the tractor which brings their hay may not respond to the sound of a landrover.

As soon as they are feeding properly, baby puppies will respond to the sound they associate with food, such as the kennel door opening – this is when a deaf puppy can often be spotted. Some breeders attract puppies by rattling the food dish, and some gun dog trainers fire a gun as a sort of dinner gong! This helps to avoid gun shyness, because the pups learn to associate gunfire with a pleasant experience.

Our own ACD puppies learn to come to "Puppy, puppy", and when they are taken out of the kennel, they will rush to Mary in response to that call. So when they go to new homes, all the new owner has to do is put the puppy's name before "puppy, puppy", and in a very short space of time the pup should be answering to its name only. We have never had puppies which learn to respond to their names as quickly as ACDs.

There are many methods by which owners teach their dogs not to come when called. One example is the owner whose puppy is pottering around the garden and suddenly decides to investigate something in the flower border. The owner shouts, and when the puppy ignores the command, he shouts even louder. However, the puppy has a good temperament, is used to noise and continues to ignore the shouting. Soon the pup loses interest in the flower border and returns to the owner. Whereupon, the pup is seized, scolded, and probably beaten for not coming when called. At least, that is what the owner thinks. But what, in fact, he has done is correct the puppy for going to him. If it has any sense – and most ACDs have a lot of sense – the pup will be very reluctant to go to the owner next time, especially if he shouts.

We could fill a book with examples of this kind of stupidity. Suffice to say that you should never, under any circumstances, correct a puppy who has come back to you, no matter how much you may feel like wringing the little blighter's neck! If a dog of any age requires correction, as dogs frequently do, go to the dog, do not call the dog to you, in order to correct.

FOOD REWARDS
In all training, we use food as a reward, and always have done so. At one time this was very frowned upon in training circles; even today there are those who claim that it represents bribery, not training. So what? Our objective in training is, firstly, to get the dog to do what we want, when we want – and quite frequently, to refrain from doing what the dog wants to do. Secondly, we want to achieve that objective with the least possible effort on our part; and thirdly, we want the dog to enjoy training as much as possible. We have found that food (which has been used by circus trainers for generations) helps to achieve all three objectives.

However, remember that the ultimate objective is a dog which obeys – food or no food.

Invaluable though it may be in the early stages, especially in teaching a puppy to come to you, the animal should never be allowed to regard food as a right. It should be given only when the dog has done something to deserve it. As training progresses, it should only be given on special occasions; when you feel your dog deserves it, not when the dog demands it.

The same applies to reward by petting and fussing. While it is true to say that it is impossible to over-reward, it is important that the reward should be earned. Some people continually pet and fuss over their dog, so when the dog does something for which a reward is deserved, there is nothing to fall back on. It is like trying to reward a dog with food when the dog has just had too much to eat. Incidentally, patting on the head is not a reward. Most dogs hate it, though many are forced to endure it.

TONE OF VOICE

Tone of voice can and should be used in rewarding and correcting. What you say is of much less importance than how you say it. When your puppy comes to you, praise in a 'coodling' tone of voice "goo-ood dog". If the pup is doing something wrong, scold with a harsh "No" or "Agh". A puppy instinctively responds to a growl from the dam, or another dog. But a dog doesn't make a lot of noise when growling. Indeed, a dog makes very little noise, but a growl has far more effect on the animals to which it is directed than yelling and shouting from some dog owners.

The puppy's instinctive reaction to tone of voice should be reinforced by association with correction and reward. If, when the pup is doing something wrong, you say "No" as you apply correction, the puppy should associate the correction with the word. Next time you utter a harsh "No", the puppy should stop doing what it was doing without the need for any more correction. Likewise the puppy should learn to associate "Good Dog", or whatever you feel like saying, with doing what you want. This enables you to praise or correct your dog whether he is doing right or wrong, even when some distance away.

LEAD TRAINING

Sooner or later your ACD will have to go on a lead. Perhaps you put a collar and lead on for the journey home from the breeder, but that was only to act as a safety line in case of emergency. Remove the collar when you get the puppy home. Most puppies dislike a collar to begin with; in a new home there will be plenty of little traumas to cope with without adding an unnecessary one.

Once the pup has settled down, you can put the collar back on, and leave it on until the pup ignores it. Make sure the collar is not too tight, but equally, it should not be too slack or the puppy may get it off, or get its bottom jaw caught in the collar in an effort to do so. Do not attempt to attach a lead until your puppy is quite happy with the collar, and you should not try a collar and lead until the puppy will follow you without one.

The lead should never be regarded as a means of making a dog go with the owner; it is only a safety line which can prevent a puppy from running away if suddenly frightened, or serve to guide a dog while teaching some new exercise. The reactions of different puppies vary enormously when first put on a lead. Most ACD puppies just trot along as they were doing before the lead was attached, and, of course, should be well rewarded for doing so. Occasionally, a puppy feels 'caught' and struggles to get away. Do not fight with the puppy. Just stand still and let the pup discover that there is no means of escaping, no matter how hard the dog tries. As soon as the puppy relaxes, give lots of praise and encourage the puppy to come with you with the aid of food.

Soon the puppy should be trotting along quite happily, so happily, in fact, that a problem could be starting – pulling on the lead, which can start much earlier than many people realise. However,

Meaghan Thacker's Ch. Quickheels Temtullens Zola, enjoying a bone. It is natural for all puppies to chew, and you should provide something suitable, such as a marrow bone or a toy for the purpose. Gnawing a bone also helps to keep the adult's teeth clean.

it takes two to pull. When the puppy pulls, give a sharp jerk on the lead; no need to jerk the pup head over heels, just give a sharp little jerk, sufficient to cause some discomfort. When the puppy responds, praise well, and offer food. The main object is to get the puppy to associate pulling with discomfort, and walking close to you with pleasure. Most dogs like pulling and it can quickly become a habit. All habits should be nipped in the bud. If this one is allowed to develop, the neck becomes hardened, like a horse with a hard mouth, and it will become progressively more difficult to apply any correction.

CHEWING

It is natural for a puppy to want to chew, and you have already been advised to provide some toys for that purpose. But it is quite likely that your puppy will find something which is deemed to be more attractive than the toys you have provided! Rugs seem to have a great fascination, and here owners often make the mistake of trying to pull the rug away from the puppy. That is just what the pup wants! This 'dead thing' which the puppy was quietly chewing suddenly comes to life, so now the pup can try to kill it. The more you pull, the more the puppy will hang on.

If your ACD is chewing something that is forbidden, take hold of the pup by the scruff, gently but firmly. Now say a harsh "No", or "Leave", and at the same time rap the puppy on the nose with your other hand. If the pup does not respond, tighten your grip on the scruff, and rap the nose a bit harder. If you have a really tough puppy, you may have to give a shake and an even firmer rap. Immediately the pup lets go, give plenty of praise and one of the permitted chewable "toys", encouraging the pup to play with that instead. Do not worry about making your ACD afraid of your hand. A bitch corrects her puppies with her teeth, but that does not make them afraid of going near her mouth.

Soon you should be able to stop the puppy chewing by simply saying "Leave!" – a command which can prove useful throughout the dog's life.

GAMES

There is no harm in playing tug-of-war games with your puppy, provided the pup leaves when you say so. In fact, this can be used as a disciplinary exercise. You encourage the puppy to play by shaking a piece of rag, rope etc., at the same time giving a command – we simply hiss "sst". When the pup is really enjoying the game, give the command to leave, and make sure the dog responds. Repeat this a few times, and then finish. Do not go on until the puppy becomes tired and wants to stop. All games should end when you say so, and not when the dog feels like it.

Many people believe they are playing with their dog when, in fact, the dog is playing with them. A typical example is the owner out walking with the dog who fetches a stick, puts it down at the owner's feet, and quite clearly says "Throw it for me". The obedient owner throws the stick, and the action is repeated over and over again, until the dog gets fed up with the game. Then, when the owner throws the stick, the dog says "I've had enough, go and fetch it yourself." The owner quite frequently obeys that too!

DOMINANCE

The sequence of events, described above, is a sure recipe for encouraging dominance, although, strangely enough, all dogs treated in this way do not become dominant. Since the advent of the professional canine behaviourist – quite a recent occurrence – we hear a lot more about dominance than we did in the past. Without in any way belittling the importance of dominance, it does seem that some behaviourists have become rather obsessive about it. If a dog owner has a problem, there seems to be a tendency to blame it on dominance, without looking for the many other possible reasons.

To understand dominance, it is necessary to learn something about the pack instinct. This is one of the dog's strongest instincts, and one which, more than any other, affects the man/dog relationship. In a pack of wild dogs there is always a leader, and usually one or two younger members of the pack with aspirations to become leader. Most groups of animals living together form a "pecking" order. 'A' chooses the best perch and the best food, and can peck any hen from 'B' downwards. 'B' can peck anyone from 'C' downwards, but not 'A', and so it goes on until we reach 'Z' who pecks no one and gets pecked by everyone! In these cases, the subordinate animals simply keep out of the way of the dominant ones, allowing them to feed first, go through doors and gates first, and choose the best places to rest.

In the dog pack, it is much more highly organised. Members of the pack not only obey the leader; they co-operate in hunting forays, and even in "domestic chores", like helping to look after the pups. If a puppy is removed from the pack when quite young, the pup should become attached to the human leader, and will be willing to obey him/her.

The pack instinct is still very strong in the domestic dog, which is very fortunate for us. That is why the dog is willing, even anxious, to accept a human master as a replacement for a canine leader. And that is why the dog is so much easier to train than the cat, which is every bit as intelligent and has been domesticated for as long, or perhaps even longer. A pack leader has to be dominant in order to lead. How dominant the leader needs to be depends on how submissive the rest of the pack is. If a dominant puppy is removed from one group, and placed with another group of the same breed and age, that pup could be well down in the hierarchy. Dominance is hereditary, which is why some breeds are, on the whole, more dominant than others.

In spite of this, some behaviourists claim that dominance is the cause of more problems than all other causes put together. This is quite possibly true, but not because dogs are any more dominant than they were some years ago. It is far more likely, in our view, that many of today's dog owners allow themselves to be dominated; they even allow their own children, of three or four years old, to dominate the household! Unlike many human parents, a bitch is never dominated by her puppies, in spite of there being a whole litter of them. If she wants a bone she takes it. If a puppy should be so rash as to try to take it from her, that pup soon regrets the action.

Yet that same puppy may go to a new home, and in no time at all, the new owner says "My dog won't let me take a bone away, or touch the feeding dish." An eight-week-old puppy, a canine baby, will not *let* an adult human being – supposed to be a "superior animal" – take its bone. To make matters worse, some people find this sort of behaviour funny and laugh at the puppy. Treating a puppy like that quickly creates a problem – a very dangerous one with a breed like the ACD, which has a strong guarding instinct and a powerful bite.

A modern school of thought has drawn up some very specific rules which, it claims, will ensure that the puppy does not dominate the owner. Right from the start, it is recommended that you take steps to ensure that the puppy understands that you are the pack leader. But a seven-week-old puppy neither needs nor wants a pack leader. What a puppy of that age misses is his Mum, who may have ticked him off when he did wrong, but who offered affection and support in times of need. As we said, not all dogs are dominant, and many puppies need someone to give them confidence rather than dominate them. Incidentally, with very few exceptions, women make very much better puppy rearers than men – we both agree on that.

Another modern idea is that the puppy must never be fed before the family – the other members of the pack. In the wild, a bitch carries food to her puppies in her stomach. It is then regurgitated for the puppies to eat when she returns to the den. The wild bitch will do that, even when she herself is starving; and when food is scarce other members of the pack will help out. We once heard Gael Fisher, the well-known American behaviourist, ask a mainly female audience who was fed first in their households. There was an unanimous chorus of "The kids".

When we rear a puppy, we always shut it in an indoor kennel to sleep. First thing in the morning, the pup is taken out with the other dogs. Once they have all relieved themselves, they come back in, and the puppy is given breakfast in the presence of the other dogs – who are not fed until after they have been exercised. The puppy is then taken out again, for toilet purposes, and then, when the pup is brought back inside, we have our own breakfast. We have lost count of the number of puppies we have reared on these lines. They have certainly included a number that have grown into very dominant dogs, including some of our best dogs. But none ever created a dominance-related problem.

We often stroke our puppies when they are feeding. If one snaps, the pup receives a sharp rap across the nose by the back of the same hand that it snapped at. If the response is a growl or a curl of the lip, we correct with a harsh "No", followed by the same treatment if the pup still ignores the warning. That is what Mum would do. If a puppy snapped at her, she would snap back *immediately*. If a puppy threatened her, she would warn the pup by growling, and if the warning was not heeded, the pup would receive the same correction.

It is very rare for a bitch to actually bite a puppy. Although she appears to bite, she really only hits the puppy with her teeth, although she may hit hard, inflicting much more pain than could be inflicted by a human hand. But that does not make the puppies dislike her, because she corrects her puppies at the right time, and *she does not nag.*

We always have a dog sleeping on the bed – very often a cat too! This is a sure way to encourage dominance in the dog, we are told. The same applies to allowing a dog to lie on the sofa, or on other furniture. The only harm we have found resulting from this is to the furniture. A similar view has been expressed by many people who regard dogs as friends as well as servants.

It should perhaps be mentioned that our dogs only get up on the furniture beside us when they are invited. If a dog gets up on its own accord, the dog is promptly told to get down again. In a short time the dog will be allowed to get back up – because we say so, not because the dog has made the decision.

There is some difference of opinion as to whether, when a dog is lying on the floor, you should make the dog get up, or step over it. Some say that making a dog get up emphasises the superiority of the pack leader. But we teach our dogs to stay still and allow us to step over them – which is surely showing our dominance and the dog's submissiveness.

A pack leader should lead. Many owners overlook that principle by allowing the dog to go through doors or gates ahead of them. Apart from encouraging dominance in the dog, it can be very dangerous, especially with an elderly owner. Attention to what appear to be small details, such as we have been describing, will do more to prevent your dog from dominating you, than letting the puppy have breakfast before you have your own.

SOCIALISATION CLASSES

Puppy socialisation classes or "puppy parties" have been a great success in the US, where they were first started by Dr Ian Dunbar, and they are now popular in the UK, and probably in some other countries too. These are not to be confused with Obedience training classes. Socialisation classes cater for puppies from any age after they have completed their vaccinations until they are six months old.

Groups of families meet with their puppies, which are allowed to play around together under supervision, but with as little interference as possible. The pups learn to go to their owners and to strangers in response to food and petting. There is already ample evidence which shows that dogs socialised in this way as puppies interact better with other dogs than those which have not been socialised. They also interact better with people, including children.

The ACD, being naturally suspicious of strangers – and not always over-friendly with other dogs – is more likely to benefit from early socialisation than some other breeds. Do not worry about your puppy losing his guarding instinct. If an instinct is there, it will make itself apparent when the occasion warrants it, even with a dog that is very friendly at all other times.

Obviously socialisation classes can only be organised where sufficient puppy owners are able and willing to meet on a fairly regular basis. In some areas this is easy; in others it is quite impossible, but it is well worthwhile making enquiries as to whether there are any in your area. If so, go along and see what is going on before you take your puppy. All classes are only as good as their instructors. In all walks of life, you find people ever-anxious to give advice who are really in need of advice themselves!

Because they vaccinate puppies, vets usually know if, and where, puppy classes are being held; some even hold classes themselves. These have the added advantage of helping the puppy to associate the vet and his surgery (which many dogs hate), with having a good time.

Chapter Eight

TRAINING YOUR ACD

PUPPY TRAINING
BASIC COMMANDS

If there are puppy socialisation classes and/or puppy playgroups in your area, do try to take your pup along. There the pup will learn how to interact with other dogs, with children and adults, and will benefit from quite a lot of early 'play training'. However, it is at home that most of the early training should be done – training that should be elementary, but fun. The pup is only young; concentration-span is very limited, but the ability to learn is considerable. If you are consistent and patient, you should find that with very little effort your ACD can soon be taught to come when called, and respond to the commands 'Sit', 'Down', and 'Stand'.

To begin with, call your puppy to you, and reward with dinner or a tidbit. Whenever you call your pup, make sure you give a reward. This does not always have to be food; sometimes you can have a game, throw a toy, or go out for a walk – it doesn't matter what, so long as the puppy receives a reward for doing the right thing. Do not keep calling your puppy for nothing – that is a sure way to teach a dog to ignore you.

To teach the command 'Sit', start by calling your ACD at mealtimes. When the puppy comes near, hold the bowl over his head, saying 'Sit'. The puppy should automatically look up and sit back on the hindquarters. Give plenty of praise – and the food. You can re-inforce this training by calling the puppy to you and then offering a tidbit, holding your hand over the dog's head, and giving the reward as soon as you get a sit. It is surprising how quickly most pups learn this way, and enjoy it too. Once your ACD is sitting promptly in response to your command, stop offering food every time. Always give plenty of praise, but make food a special reward to be given at irregular intervals.

Your puppy can be taught the 'Down' in a similar manner. Command your ACD to sit, and hold a tidbit in your hand. Then, lower your hand to the ground, just in front of the puppy's nose. If the pup makes a rush forward, restrain with your other hand. Never give the reward until the puppy is in the correct position. The 'Stand' can be taught from either the 'Sit' or the 'Down'. Hold the food in front of the pup, level with the head. Do not let the puppy grab at it; wait until you have a proper stand, before you give the reward. If necessary, restrain your puppy with your other hand. With any exercise, it is a good idea to teach the pup a 'release' command. Use any word you like – we use 'OK', which means exercise finished. Do not try making a pup do long 'Stays'; a minute is sufficient, as long as the pup is staying happily, and this will lay a good foundation for more advanced work.

If you have ambitions for Obedience training, you can teach the beginning of a 'Send away' at this stage. Put the food bowl down in the kitchen, and show it to your ACD. Then, take your puppy back to the door. Give the command 'Go', and let the pup run to the food. Once your puppy has the idea, you can continue with lesson, using tidbits out in the garden and in other places. This is also a good time to introduce the 'Leave' command. If a pup is taught early on to leave food until told to have it, it should be much easier, at a later stage, to check your ACD from picking up rubbish on walks, or tidbits that have been dropped in the show ring. The command 'Leave', can also be used to stop your ACD running up to strange dogs. Start by giving the command 'Sit'; put food down, and keep your puppy in the sitting position (use a lead, if necessary), and give the command 'Leave'. The pup may be a bit confused to begin with, so do not keep on too long. As soon as your puppy is staying quietly, give the command 'Take it', and give plenty of praise. You can then do the same thing with a biscuit in your hand, or on the ground.

Puppies can be taught to sit as early as six weeks.

Most pups love playing with toys, balls etc., and this is the time to encourage your pup to retrieve. Pick a favourite toy, and throw it for your puppy. Encourage the pup to retrieve, by running away and calling your puppy excitedly. Decide on a command to use; do not use it when you are playing, only use it you when you want your puppy to bring something back to you. Do not go on too long, or the pup will get fed up. However, make sure that *you* decide when to stop, and put the toy away.

HOUSE MANNERS
Your ACD must also learn 'house manners'. A puppy must learn to be left alone – which is where a crate comes in useful. It is also useful if your dog accepts being tied up, as you never know when this might be necessary. Tie you puppy up when you are working in the kitchen or garden – a familiar place, where you can still be in sight. Always use a line or a light chain, with a swivel that turns freely. If your puppy reacts by struggling, do not take any notice. As soon as the pup settles down, go and give plenty of praise, and then let your pup go free. Gradually increase the time you leave the puppy tied up, and then start going out of sight when you leave your puppy.

If you are taking your ACD to puppy classes, this will give the opportunity to meet children. Of course, if you have a family of your own, your puppy will be used to children and their friends. Whatever your circumstances, you must get your puppy the chance to grow up knowing children – so if you have none, beg, borrow or steal some!

Most dogs travel around with the family in the car, and in this situation good behaviour is very important. If you have a crate, put your ACD in it. Teach the pup to stay quietly when left. If you hear barking, try to creep back without being seen, and then you can correct *while your puppy is barking*. Then go away again and hide round the corner. If the puppy is quiet, go back and give plenty of praise. Never let your ACD get into or out of the car, unless told to do so. A dog that rushes out of a car is a danger to everyone, and could easily be run over.

FURTHER TRAINING
APPROACH TO TRAINING

As already mentioned, all training is based on correction and reward. Until quite recently the emphasis was on correction. The dog was allowed, even encouraged to do the wrong thing so that it could be corrected. The use of a chain choke collar and a six foot long lead was almost universal in Obedience training circles. When teaching heelwork, the dog was allowed to run ahead of the handler, who would say "Heel", turn sharply to the right, and give the dog a mighty jerk on the collar. When, in response to this correction, the dog came close to the handler, reward was given by tone of voice and caressing on the cheek with the left hand. The use of food was frowned upon, and one very well-known trainer described it as "the last resort of the incompetent". Training did not start until the puppy was six months old.

All this has changed, or, more accurately, is changing, as there are still a lot of people who stick to the old methods. But as with all changes there is always a tendency to go to the other extreme. A 'lure-reward' training system is now recommended. According to its advocates, no correction is necessary, and a puppy trained on the lines described at the beginning of this chapter, will be no trouble for the rest of its life! Perhaps not, but this theory overlooks one important fact. Like ourselves, puppies grow up, and as they grow up, their instincts develop. These instincts frequently urge the dog to do something which the owner considers undesirable. It was the late Barbara Woodhouse who said: "You can't compete with a smell on a gatepost."

A fact overlooked by those who decry what they describe as the 'stomp and jerk' system of training is that over the years and throughout the world, hundreds and thousands of dogs have been trained on that principle. These include police dogs, service dogs, guide dogs and many more. We ourselves have trained many dogs on the same principle. Quite a number of these dogs would have been euthanatised had we not been able to achieve a certain degree of control. We do not claim that all these dogs enjoyed every minute of their training; but we have no doubts that the vast majority enjoyed a better quality of life than dogs which have no training at all.

However, although we believed in the old-fashioned principles, we never did approve of some of the methods by which those principles were applied. Experience taught us that some dogs respond much better to an ordinary buckled collar than to the 'essential' chain choke collar. We have also used, with success, what is called a 'pinch collar' in the US. This is widely available in the US and in most European countries, but not in the UK, where it is called a 'spike collar' and regarded as an instrument of torture by many people. So the right or wrong method of training can depend on where you live!

THE NEED FOR CORRECTION

It has always been our opinion that puppies could learn much earlier than most people imagined. It was even more obvious that by six months of age an untrained puppy could be a real problem. Much as we approve of training young puppies by reward only, in the majority of cases there comes a time when that training will have to be reinforced by correction. But that correction will be much easier to apply, and much kinder to the puppy, if the basic commands are understood. Many people say their dog is disobedient when, in fact, they have failed or not bothered to teach the dog what is required.

THE STAY

If you have trained your ACD by reward only, the commands to come, sit, stand and lie down, should be understood. You will know this when your pup responds before the reward is given. The puppy should also have learned a command to stay when you go through a door or get out of the car. By combining the two commands, you can now teach the pup to stay when you move away. Eventually your ACD should stay in the stand, sit or down position, but most dogs will stay more readily in the last position than in the other two. Give the command 'Down', and when the pup is in position, give the command 'Stay'. Now, take a few steps back, pause for a short while, return to the pup and give plenty of praise. Repeat the process, but next time go a little further. Although easy to teach, young puppies, like small children, cannot concentrate for any length of time.

As your ACD gets older, you should very gradually increase the distance you move away, and the length of time you leave your dog. Move to either side and around the back of the puppy, and keep going back to praise. Some people sit the dog, and after the stay, they give the command to come, and then praise the dog. This is something we would never do. When we are teaching a dog to stay on command, we reward the dog for staying. Never call from the 'Down', until you are confident that the dog is quite steady on that exercise.

If the puppy does move, you will have to use correction. Do not wait until the pup comes to you. As soon as the puppy breaks the stay, respond quickly and quietly by taking hold of the collar, and putting the pup back on the exact spot he has left. Try to give the impression that you are very angry. Of course, you must not be angry – and do not forget that correction which would really upset one ACD may be treated as something of a joke by another. When you have put the puppy back in place, give the command to stay, and move away again. Do not go as far away as the last time, and only leave your pup for a very short time. Then return, reward the puppy, give the 'release' command, and finish for the day. Tomorrow you can start where you left off, thus avoiding the risk of your puppy disliking the exercise, or even disliking you for repeating the lesson over and over again.

In all training, every exercise should end on a good note, with the dog doing what is required. If your ACD sits for two minutes and gets up when you say so, you have gone a step forward. If your dog sits for two hours, and then gets up when he feels like it, you have gone a step backwards – probably a very big step.

DROP ON COMMAND

Governments in all parts of the world seem to be determined to bring in legislation designed to make life as difficult as possible for dogs and their owners. This makes it more essential than ever to keep our dogs under control at all times. To achieve this, there are two vital exercises. Firstly the dog must come when called, and secondly the dog must 'drop' on command – and stay there. The latter is, in our opinion, even more important than the former.

A dog that is lying down cannot bite a jogger passing by, nor jump up and leave muddy paw marks on a friend's best clothes. There cannot possibly be "grounds for reasonable apprehension" that a dog, controlled in this way, will injure anyone – which, in the UK, would render it liable to be killed under the Dangerous Dogs Act 1991. If a dog takes off after something, it is usually easier to get the dog to drop, than to expect a U-turn when the dog is in full flight. If the dog is on the other side of the road when a car approaches, the 'drop' command might save the dog's life, until the car has passed.

To be effective, it is not sufficient for your ACD to lie down quietly and stay there while you walk away. The dog must drop instantly at any time, and in any place. At the beginning, you went back to the puppy, to reward for staying. Once your dog knows what to do, you can give the command to come from the 'Down'. Once the dog responds to the command, it is really a question of practice, which can easily be combined with exercise. When you are out for a walk and the dog is running ahead, suddenly command 'Down', keep walking until you catch up with your dog, give plenty of praise, and continue your walk together.

Alternatively, you can call your ACD to you, and give the 'drop' command halfway. Never work to a routine – that applies to all training. On the occasions when it is really necessary to drop your dog, there will be no warning. By alternating dropping on command with other activities, like chasing a stick or ball, it can become a game which is enjoyed by most dogs. If your dog is keen on retrieving a ball you can use it for practising the drop on command. Make the dog sit or lie down beside you, and throw the ball. Send the dog, give the command to drop halfway, and then send the dog on to retrieve the ball. Do not try this until your ACD is really keen on retrieving, as there is a risk that the dog may get the wrong association and think it is wrong to chase a ball.

THE HUNTING INSTINCT

Every dog has the right to run free for some part of every day. With a dog that has a tendency to chase, diligence is essential. If some 'quarry' unexpectedly appears, drop your ACD before he takes off, and give the command to stay there, until the jogger or whatever has passed. Then reward your dog, and continue your walk.

Whether or not you can stop a dog that wants to chase something is not entirely dependent on your skill as a trainer. Here we have two entirely different instincts working in conjunction with each other. The hunting instinct drives the dog on, without the dog knowing why, just as the instinct to survive makes the newly-born puppy squirm around to find a teat. This is balanced, to some extent, by the submissive instinct which makes the dog want to please the leader.

If your ACD's hunting instinct is below average strength, it is quite possible that the dog will drop immediately when you shout 'Down', even if something 'tempting' has been spotted – and you would probably be congratulating yourself on your good training. However, if the hunting instinct is very strong, and the submissive instinct is weak, the chances are that your ACD would not even falter in the mad rush towards the 'quarry' – and your friends would say you were a bad trainer! Apart from helping to control the hunting instinct, training actually strengthens the submissive instinct. The more a dog learns, the easier it becomes to teach something new. It does not matter what you teach: anything your dog does in response to your command will strengthen the submissive instinct.

THE RETRIEVE

So far, the training we have discussed has been mostly negative, which also applies to most of the tests in Obedience classes and trials. A dog that sits on command not only takes up a sitting position, but also refrains from going off to do something he would much rather do. Besides being negative, many of the exercises are repeated over and over again, so that they become boring. The working Cattle Dog is doing something positive, and is rewarded by following the working instinct. The work also provides an outlet for the ACD's exceptional energy and initiative. In our opinion, anyone who cannot, or will not, provide an alternative for all that energy, should not keep an ACD – or any other active breed for that matter. There is absolutely no reason why an individual cannot teach an ACD to use some of the other instincts which will provide both mental and physical exercise. Apart from going to ground after a fox, I can think of few tasks that any breed of dog could do, that an ACD could not manage. Nearly all dogs of all breeds have some retrieving instinct, which arises from the hunting instinct, and varies between breeds. It is not so strong in the ACD as in the Gundog breeds, but we have never had any problems teaching our dogs to retrieve, and we have not heard of anyone who has.

Retrieving, in its many forms, can provide a great deal of pleasure for both dog and trainer – and can, on occasion, be of great practical value. This instinct often shows in very young puppies who pick things up and carry them about. This is when many owners make a big mistake by scolding or even punishing when a new shoe is selected for this treatment. As we have said, instincts develop with use and can weaken, or even die out, when not used. This is even more likely to happen when the instinct is inhibited, especially when it first makes an appearance. It is a bit like a seedling which is quite delicate when it first appears. Stamp on it and that's that! Nurture it carefully and it will become stronger, and gradually it will be more difficult to damage.

The same applies to instincts. Those we want should be encouraged, and those which we do not want should be discouraged, right from the first time they make an appearance. So, if your ACD brings you some object in triumph, take it gently and praise generously. If the object is something you would rather the puppy did not have, put it quietly out of reach. If it is one of your puppy's toys, accept it and throw it for your pup to fetch. Being part of the hunting instinct, the retrieving instinct will be strengthened if you throw the object for the puppy to chase. However, do not keep on and on until the puppy gets fed up; as we have said before, always stop when the puppy is asking for more.

Do not despair if your ACD shows little interest to start with. The age at which instincts start to develop varies enormously between individuals. Some puppies will pick up anything they can get hold of by the time they are six weeks old. Others of the same litter may not show any interest until they are four or five months. The important thing is to encourage the puppy right from the very first time the interest in retrieving becomes apparent. Several dogs we have known were keen to retrieve as puppies, but were not encouraged, or were perhaps discouraged. In these cases, by the time the dog was eighteen months old, all interest in retrieving had gone.

Some of the dogs John trained by the German or Forcing method, as it is known in the UK (described fully in *The Family Dog* and *The Obedient Dog*), and they made very good retrievers. However, most of them would have been just as good if they had been taught in play, right from the start. Teaching the retrieve in play will take longer, but will usually be just as reliable in the end. It is also much easier for the novice, and much better fun for both dog and trainer. You cannot *make* a dog retrieve by this method. All you can do is encourage the dog, and hope that the retrieving instinct becomes strong enough to make the dog want to retrieve. That is likely to happen with the vast majority of ACDs.

THE SEEK BACK

There is no end to the uses to which the retrieve can be put, most of them of considerable practical value and easy to teach. The 'Seek Back' can be taught by simply dropping a glove, or any other convenient object when out for a walk. The dog must not see you drop it, but to start with, it should be in sight when you send the dog back for it. Gradually increase the distance, and drop the object in long grass, and any dog with a good nose will seek back virtually any distance.

John once exercised several dogs in a public park, and on returning to the car, he found that he had lost his car keys. Assuming he had dropped them where they had been walking, John sent 'Flush', a Cocker Spaniel, to find them. In spite of the fact that there were several other people exercising dogs in the park, Flush had little difficulty in finding the keys and bringing them back in triumph. On another occasion, the petrol cap fell off our Landrover. We heard it hit the road and stopped to look for it, but it had, apparently, bounced into thick vegetation by the roadside, and we could not find it. So we went home and returned with 'Ben', a Springer/Beardie, and he went straight in and picked it up!

As a means of exercising a dog, retrieving can save an owner a lot of walking. You can make a dog retrieve over a fallen tree, a gate, a park seat or any other obstacle that appears. The easiest way to encourage a dog to swim is to throw something that floats into a pond. A dog which will not retrieve on land, will often retrieve out of water. A lazy way of exercising is to use a tennis racket to bat balls far further than you could throw them. This exercise can also be used to improve control. Command your ACD to sit or lie down beside you, and bat out three or four tennis balls in different directions. Then send the dog to fetch each ball, in the order you request. If your dog goes for the wrong ball, stop the dog, and redirect to the right one. This will teach the dog not only to listen to you, but also to go in the direction in which you signal.

Playing tennis with your dog provides training, fun and exercise.   *Sally Anne Thompson.*

COMPETITIONS

For those of a competitive nature, there is a large number of activities popular with the dog fraternity worldwide. As the number is continually being added to, and as different countries have different rules for the same competition, we shall not go into details. Nearly all competitive activities are organised by clubs, which are usually controlled by the governing body of each country or state. So our advice to those who wish to compete in Obedience, Working Trials, Agility, Flyball, Sent Hurdling, Schutzhund, or any of the new disciplines, is to start by finding out where your nearest club operates. Then go along, without a dog, and find out what sort of people run it. Any training club is only as good as the instructor. Most are very good – but by no means all!

THE HEELING INSTINCT

As previously mentioned, the instincts which have made the ACD such an asset to mankind can, and frequently do, create problems. One example is the instinct to heel, which has made the Cattle Dog such a good worker of cattle. But if there are no cattle around, the well-bred ACD is likely to look around for a substitute. That substitute is often right there in the form of human ankles. This has nothing to do with aggression, or with the dog disliking humans; ACD puppies heel each other. Nor is it peculiar to the breed, as we well know from considerable experience with Welsh Corgis. This instinct often makes itself apparent in quite young puppies, and it is very unwise to expect your puppy to "grow out of it". We know that instincts strengthen with use, but when it is directed at the wrong 'victim', it should be firmly stamped on, right at the beginning. The big mistake many people make is to behave like a cow by trying to kick the puppy, or run away from it. Most puppies heel when excited, so the first step is to calm the situation. Stand still and do not shout, or, worse still, scream. Instead, utter a harsh "No", followed by reward when the puppy gives up the idea. It may be necessary to grab the puppy by the scruff and give a good shake.

Do not, on any account, treat it as a joke if the pup bites another member of the family! The puppy is amusing himself, and if the 'pack' show signs of being amused, the pup will enjoy it all the more. If this is nipped in the bud, it is unlikely to develop into a serious problem. If it is allowed to develop it can become a very serious problem indeed. Do not worry about inhibiting the pup, if, later on, you want to use the dog to heel cattle. An ACD knows the difference between a cow and a human, and will always prefer the heel of the former to that of the latter.

LIVING WITH OTHER ANIMALS

The historians, who must always have a reason for everything, tell us that Dalmatian blood was introduced into the ACD to give the breed "a love of horses". If "loving" means biting them on the heel, then the historians are correct! Nevertheless, for anyone who rides, an ACD is the ideal companion, and it is well worth the trouble of teaching your dog not to heel your horse.

The saying that familiarity breeds contempt is very true. A puppy allowed to potter round the stable yard before being old enough to be taken out riding will probably grow up to ignore horses – more or less! The same applies to cats, poultry, and any other domestic animals which are allowed the run of the yard. It is advisable to start a young dog with a horse that is used to dogs and is unlikely to kick. Apart from the risk of injuring the dog, an ACD is almost certain to react to the challenge by biting the offending heel. This will not help to establish an amicable dog/horse relationship, and can be disastrous with a young horse. It will also encourage the dog to heel again.

We like our dogs to run alongside a horse or just ahead of it, where they can be seen. But some dogs, especially ACDs, like to run behind. We carry a hunting whip and, with a young dog, we swing it round behind the horse to discourage the dog from getting too close to the heels. We have never had any real problems with our ACDs heeling horses, but have heard of some owners who have. Our ACDs certainly prefer cattle to horses. We graze cattle and ponies together, and all our ACDs have gone straight past the ponies, or even through a group of them, to reach the cattle. However, if there were no cattle they would be quite happy to work the ponies, although we never allow them to do so, and have no problem in stopping them.

Chapter Nine

CARING FOR YOUR ACD

Australian Cattle Dogs are generally a tough, 'no nonsense' breed, with very few hang-ups, and a coat that is easy to look after. However, there is more to looking after a dog properly than giving a quick brush, a meal, and a walk round the block!

FEEDING

Starting with a puppy at seven or eight weeks of age, you will soon be able to cut the feeds to three a day, and to two meals a day by six months. After that, it is up to you whether you prefer to feed one or two meals a day. We usually give a dry biscuit for breakfast, and one main meal. Everyone has different ideas about feeding, but so long as the correct amount is fed, it is doubtful whether the dog minds how often or when!

It is often said that a dog *must* be fed at regular times, and although this may be easiest for both dog and owner, there will always be times when it is not possible to feed at the usual time. The dog is an adaptable and accommodating creature, and it will do no harm at all to feed at irregular intervals. If, for instance, you want to take your pup out in the car and a meal is nearly due, it is better to wait and feed when you get back. If you do feed before your outing, the puppy could well be car-sick, and then you will have to feed again, on your return.

There are innumerable commercial diets on the market. The good-quality ones have an analysis on the packet, and you can see that they contain all the minerals, protein, carbohydrates, trace elements etc. in the right proportions. If you are feeding a complete diet, do not rush out and buy extra vitamins and tonics; they will do more harm than good. The dog simply does not need them, whatever the adverts say! Remember, if you are feeding a dry food, water should be available at all times.

If you prefer to feed a homemade diet, then there are a number of items to be found in most kitchens which can be used. Cereals, rice, brown bread, eggs, cheese, milk, fish (canned or fresh), and so on. Or you may decide to stick to the tried and tested 'old-fashioned' diet of biscuit meal and either raw or cooked meat. In either of these last two feeding methods, it would be advisable to check if vitamin and mineral supplements are needed.

Old dogs, like puppies, do better on several small meals per day, rather than one large one. They often need extra calcium and fewer calories to keep them fit and active. Some dogs which tend to be 'hyper-active' can benefit from a change of diet, such as one with a lower protein content and/or free from additives.

Avoid giving tidbits, except as a reward. Never feed the dog at mealtimes. If you cannot stop the family feeding the dog under the table, banish either the dog or the family to the kitchen! Always

ACDs are a tough, no-nonsense breed. Dutch Ch. Formakin Boomer, aged ten years, just emerged from a swim.

remember that the ACD was specifically bred to work long, hard hours under harsh conditions. This dog never knew when the next meal would be coming – or whether it was coming at all! Consequently, when kept under modern so-called 'improved conditions', the majority of the breed tend to put on weight very easily, unless they are sensibly fed and well exercised. It is always easier to put weight on a dog than to take it off.

In fact, it would do your dog no harm, and probably a lot of good, if you only fed six days a week. It is quite natural for a carnivore (and although omnivorous in many ways, a dog is primarily a carnivore) to eat at irregular intervals. In the wild, wolves only eat when they have managed to catch their dinner – which may be two days running, or they may not eat for several days. In most zoos wolves are only fed three or four times a week.

For many years now we have only fed our dogs six days a week – on Sundays they are not fed at all. This not only does them good and gives their stomachs a rest, but also gives us a break from preparing food on that day. If you have any 'poor doers' in your kennel (very unlikely with ACDs), you will find that after a day without food even fussy feeders eat up on Mondays. We would add that both puppies and old dogs do have a small feed on Sundays.

BEDDING

Once the pup has stopped growing, you can decide on what sort of bed you want to buy. Pet shops and trade stands at dog shows are crowded with luxurious beds, baskets and everything else you can imagine. Baskets are not a good idea. They are draughty, collect dirt, and they are very chewable! Bean bags are popular with dogs and owners, and can be used in the dog crate when travelling. Fleece bedding is soft, hygienic and washable.

Never put a wet dog to bed, and be careful where you put the bed at night. If the dog has been lying in front of a blazing fire or a hot radiator, a hall, with a howling gale blowing under the door, will be a most unpleasant contrast. Your dog's bed should be located somewhere warm and draughtproof. Old dogs often feel the cold and need really warm, comfortable beds. Small heated pads are often very useful for old dogs who have a bit of rheumatism.

GROOMING

Grooming your ACD will not be a time-consuming job, but this does not mean that your dog does not need grooming. It is wise to start these sessions at the puppy stage, and get your dog used to lying, sitting, lying on one side, and standing on a table in order to be brushed.

You will need a good stiff, bristle brush and a steel comb. A pup actually needs little grooming, but this is the ideal time to accustom your dog to being handled. If you teach your dog to behave at an early age, you will reap the benefits in the show ring, or when your dog is examined by the vet.

Start off by teaching your puppy to keep still while you run your hands over the coat. Examine the mouth, pick up each foot in turn, inspect the ears. To begin with, the pup will almost certainly squirm and wriggle. Keep talking to your puppy, while taking a firm but gentle hold. Once your dog has relaxed, give plenty of praise, and then reward with a game.

There are occasions when another couple of grooming aids may be useful. A chamois leather – or the synthetic type which will do the job just as well – can be a great help to give the coat a final polish; or it can be used in wet, dirty weather to dry the dog off. You will find it much better than a towel.

The other item is a good-quality wire dog-brush. You will need this when the dog sheds coat – usually, but not always, twice a year. Bitches will always shed their coats soon after the puppies are weaned. Although both sexes shed, the dogs do not go in for it so wholeheartedly as the bitches! When a bitch loses her coat, she really makes a job of it, and looks like a 'skinned rabbit'. All the soft, fluffy undercoat will fall out, but with a little help from you, the process can be speeded up quite a lot.

When you see the tell-tale signs of clumps of soft hair all over the place, it is time to get hold of the dog and do something about it. This is when the wire brush is used. You can also use the comb on the tail and the longer hair on the breeching, but we find a wire brush gets the coat out much more easily. If it is the first time your ACD has shed its coat, you will probably be amazed, and possibly horrified, at how much hair comes out. Do not worry, it will soon grow back in again.

After you have got out as much undercoat as possible, the next thing is to give the dog a thorough bath to remove the rest of the loose hair. After the dog is dry, give another brushing and, with any luck, you will have got the worst of the old coat out. Continue brushing daily for as long as it takes to get rid of all the old coat. All this will help the new coat to come through fairly quickly.

Feeding is very important at this time. Most dogs, in fact, most animals and birds lose condition when changing coats or feathers. So make sure you feed a good-quality food, and add a little extra oil. Margarine, cooking oil or such-like are suitable. Seaweed, in the form of powder or tablets, is also a useful addition to the diet, and promotes good coat growth.

ADMINISTERING MEDICINES

This is also the time to teach your dog to take medicine. If this procedure is accepted at the puppy stage, it will be much easier for all concerned if the dog is ever ill. A struggling, frightened dog is not a good patient. Equip yourself with some small, round candies, liver treats, choc drops, or something similar, and give the pup a couple to eat. Then, put your hand over the dog's muzzle, lift the head up slightly, pull the lips down over the top teeth and press inwards, keeping the lips between the fingers and teeth. This should cause the dog to open its mouth. As soon as this happens, pop a 'pill' right at the back of the dog's tongue, shut the mouth and gently massage the throat until the dog has swallowed it. Follow this up by letting the dog eat a treat, and then repeat the process. Most dogs will soon get the hang of it, and will quite enjoy the 'pill popping' session.

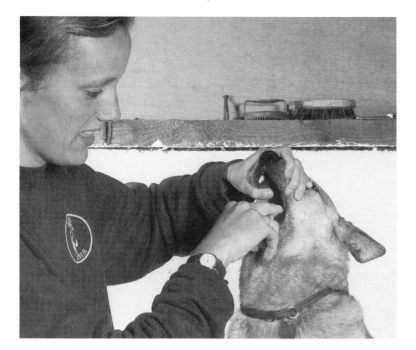

LEFT: The correct way to give a pill.

BELOW: A syringe can be helpful when giving your dog liquid medicine.

Sally Anne Thompson.

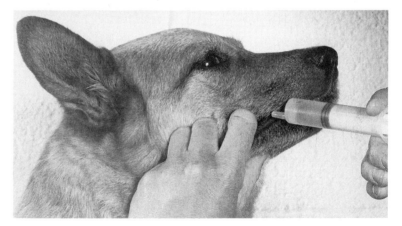

Liquid medicine is best given with someone holding the dog in a sitting position, and using either plain water or something palatable, like milk. A small, plastic bottle or a hypodermic syringe, without the needle, are both useful for liquid medicine. Insert a finger gently between the teeth and cheek and pull the bottom lip out until a pouch is formed. Keep the head steady and slowly pour the liquid into the pouch, keeping the head slightly tilted upwards. Medicine is always better given in the above ways, rather than in the food. If the dog does not eat up, you have no idea how much medicine has been taken.

TAKING YOUR DOG'S TEMPERATURE
This is another procedure you can teach when you are grooming your puppy. If you ring your vet

to say the dog is ill, you will almost certainly be asked what the dog's temperature is. A dog that has never had its temperature taken can object quite strongly to this procedure, not surprisingly!

Use a snub-nosed thermometer, shake it down before use, and put a dab of petroleum jelly or oil on the end. Enlist the help of a friend to hold the dog in a standing position, and then hold up the tail and insert the thermometer gently into the rectum. Hold it there for the required time, gently withdraw it, wipe it clean and read the temperature. A normal temperature is 38.61C. Always hold the thermometer firmly – it has been known for it to completely vanish into the rectum.

TEETH
Dogs collect tartar on their teeth, just as we do. This can cause bad breath and loose teeth. Wild dogs have the advantage of regularly chewing on bones, thus helping to keep the teeth clean. With the modern diets we have today, the teeth tend to collect more tartar. If you give your dog large marrow bones, or hard, good-quality rubber balls or other toys, it can help alleviate this problem.

Removing tartar with a tooth-scraper.

Sally Anne Thompson.

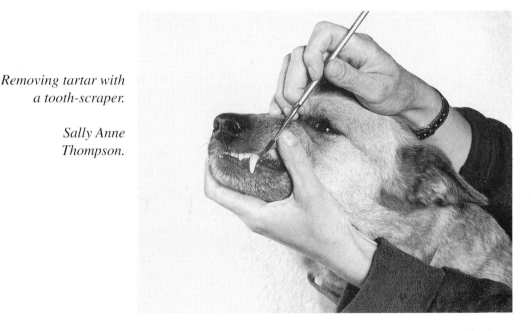

Plaque can be removed from the teeth by brushing, and most pet stores now sell 'doggy toothpaste' and brushes. If you prefer a simpler method, a piece of rough gauze, soaked in saline solution or bicarbonate of soda, will make a good job of it. The tartar is more difficult to dislodge, but this can be done with a tooth scraper. Be very gentle when using this, and push the gum well back so that you do not damage it.

NAILS
There are numerous types of nail-clippers on the market. Nearly all do a good job, so use the ones with which you feel most comfortable. We usually use a guillotine type for our ACDs. When a dog is standing naturally, the nails should just touch the ground; long nails cause a dog to move badly and tend to spread the foot. Most ACDs have good tight feet, but, even so, if only exercised on soft ground a dog's nails will need cutting from time to time. It is worth buying a good quality pair of

If nail-trimming is introduced from an early age, your dog should learn to accept the procedure.

Sally Anne Thompson.

It is often easier to turn the foot upwards.

Sally Anne Thompson.

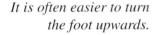

clippers as they will last longer and do a better job. You will find a coarse nail-file useful to finish off with. Once again, get your puppy used to this procedure from an early stage. Some dogs dislike the operation intensely, so the sooner you start the better. In light-coloured nails, the quick can be seen as a small pink line running down the nail. Be careful not to cut this, as it will not only hurt the dog, but will also bleed profusely. On dark nails, where the quick is not so easily seen, it is often easier to turn the foot up and cut the nails from the underside. Do not forget the dewclaws, found on the inside of the front leg a short way up from the foot. If left, these can grow into the leg and cause abscesses.

BATHING

Most ACDs love swimming, and it is an excellent form of exercise   *Sally Anne Thompson.*

Nobody likes a dirty, smelly dog around the house. So how often should you bathe your ACD? The short answer is, as often as necessary. A working dog you will probably keep clean by bathing in the horse trough, in the river, or in the creek. However, there will be many occasions when a pet or show dog needs a bath.

Pick a warm day, if possible, and use a dog shampoo – not just any old detergent from the kitchen sink. Place the dog in the bath, the sink, or whatever you are using, with just a little water, making sure the water is not too warm. Pour the shampoo on to the dog, and work this up into a good lather. Leave the head until last: once the head is wet, the dog will try to shake – and will probably succeed.

Be careful not to get shampoo in the eyes or the ears. Once the dog is well washed, pour water all over the body until all the lather is completely rinsed out. Slip a lead on, and let your dog have a good shake. Do not let your dog run loose; most dogs will invariably head for the nearest muddy patch, and roll. Give a good rub with a rough towel, and then take your dog for a brisk walk.

EXERCISE

Puppies do not need to be taken for long walks, but they do need plenty of exercise. If you have a large garden, and plenty of toys, and maybe a 'digging pit', the pup will take quite a lot of exercise playing there. However, few pups will play on their own, and so you are going to have to join in the games. Sensible walks are OK. A potter in the woods or fields for an hour or so, letting the pup run free at its own pace, and having the occasional rest, will be beneficial both physically and mentally – a five mile hike, at four miles an hour, will not!

Once mature, we have found that nearly all ACDs are virtually tireless. We used to take the ACDs out in the forest when we were horse-riding, going most days for anything from one to two hours, and the dogs always came back asking for more! Teaching your ACD to jump, swim, play frisbees, retrieve and search for lost articles, all provide different means of exercise. Nearly all

ACDs love swimming, which is excellent exercise for them, and is easy on the owner.

VACCINATIONS

These vary according to different countries, but most dogs are now vaccinated against distemper, hepatitis, leptospirosis, hard pad and parvovirus. A rabies vaccination is required by law in most countries where rabies is endemic. Generally speaking, dogs are resistant to tetanus, but it can occur, usually in country districts. Your vet will know if protection is necessary. There are also tick-borne diseases in some countries, and dogs can be vaccinated against these. Adult dogs will require booster vaccinations, and this is a matter you should discuss with your own vet.

WORMS *(Contributed by Meyrick Stephens, B. Sc., MRCVS)*
ROUNDWORMS

To start at the beginning, it is necessary to look at the pregnant bitch and the new-born puppy. When a bitch is pregnant, the worm we are concerned with is the roundworm, toxocara canis, and to be able to control this worm in puppies we need to understand its life cycle.

An adult dog does not normally have significant numbers of adult roundworms in the bowel. Nevertheless, the infective eggs are picked up from the environment. In the adult dog, the eggs hatch in the intestines and the larvae pass through the bowel, liver and lungs to become dormant in the muscle. They will survive there for more than three years. When a bitch becomes pregnant, these larvae become active after the forty-second day. They will then pass through the placenta and infect the liver and lungs of the puppy foetus.

When the puppy is born, these larvae migrate up the trachea and are swallowed. Mature worms can be present in the puppies' bowels as early as two weeks old. If the bitch picks up more worm eggs later in pregnancy, or in early lactation, larvae can be passed in the milk up to the fourth week of lactation. Because of the migration of the larvae, the puppy will not only have large numbers of worms in the bowel but tissue damage and pneumonia can also occur.

Study of this life cycle gives us the best methods to control the problem. Obviously, it is essential to lower the contamination in the environment. Worming the bitch during her pregnancy is vital. The piperazine wormers are very effective against adult worms in the bowel, but this does not remove the larvae from the muscle. The only drug which can control this is fenbendazole (panacur) given daily from the fortieth day of pregnancy until the third week of lactation. Unfortunately, this is expensive, and cannot, even then, completely eliminate the problem.

Therefore, worming of puppies should start at two weeks old, and because the bitch may be re-infecting herself as she cleans up the puppies, she should be wormed at the same time. Obviously, we need to ensure the health of our dogs, particularly puppies, but our other concern is to try to remove the risk of toxocaris infection in humans. The number of diagnosed cases is very few per annum, but a far higher percentage have serological evidence of infection; so the risk is present and must be more so with close contact with dogs.

Puppies should be wormed at two, four, six, eight and twelve weeks, because during this period worms will develop to reactivate egg-laying in the adult. The bitch should be wormed at the same intervals. This is often neglected, but since the bitch is out and about, she constitutes a greater risk to the environment. From this time the normal, regular worming for all worms should be adopted.

Although adult dogs do not harbour large numbers of roundworms, ten to twenty per cent of dogs do have mature toxocara in the bowel. There is a rise in the number of eggs passed by bitches after being in season, so it is advisable to worm at the beginning of heat. How can the contamination to the environment be controlled? The eggs, when passed, have a sticky coat which will adhere to any surface. They are resistant to all disinfectants, and will live for a year in compost. They die on hot, dry concrete, but live up to three years in moist grass. The only sure way to kill toxocara eggs in faeces is by burning. Eggs may be eaten by small rodents and remain a potential source of infection – another reason to control vermin.

There are a number of other roundworms which may be a problem. In the dog the important ones (apart from toxocara) are the Hookworm, the Whipworm, the Lungworm and the Heartworm.

THE HOOKWORM: Unicinaria Stenocephala is most common in intensive situations such as hunt or Greyhound kennels, but is not very common except in Northern Ireland. The larvae gain entrance by ingestion, or through the feet when pedal eczema occurs. It will pass through bitch's milk, when it causes illness in very young puppies, which is difficult to control. There is a much more pathogenic Hookworm, U. caninum, which causes severe anaemia, but this is only seen in dogs imported from the tropics.

THE WHIPWORM: Trichuris vulpis is unusual as it lives in the large intestine. The larvae are infective as soon as they are passed, so heavy infections are possible, which cause watery diarrhoea. Eggs can survive for up to five years, and the infection is usually associated with grass paddocks.

THE LUNGWORM: Filaroides osteri is not common and is seldom serious, but is difficult to eradicate. A deep rasping cough is caused, with sputum containing larvae produced. Infection can be passed to puppies by bitches when cleaning them.

THE HEARTWORM: Dirofilaria Immitis is not endemic to the UK; however, it is common in many countries including Australasia and North America. The disease can be dangerous as certain major organs can be damaged before detection. The disease is carried by mosquitoes which have bitten infected animals. Clinical signs of the disease include tiredness, coughing and shortness of breath. If you live in an area where heartworms are rife you should consult your vet before giving any medication. Your dog can be put on a preventative programme which includes regular dosing and your vet will advise you about this.

TAPEWORMS

Tapeworm infestation seems to hold more terror for dog owners than roundworms. Perhaps this is because the infective segments, like celery seeds or active grains of rice, can be seen round the anus or faeces. But unless the number of worms becomes large, they are not likely to affect the health of the dog. However, they are unpleasant, they can cause loss of condition and digestive upset, and they have an unpleasant public health significance.

In the UK there are three species of tapeworms affecting dogs. They all have the same type of life cycle, which is that infection does not go directly from dog to dog, but requires development in a secondary host. The hosts are significantly different in each species.

DIPYLIDIUM CANINUM: This is the most common tapeworm of dogs. It can grow more than eighteen inches in length, and its intermediate host is the flea or louse. The flea larvae of the dog, cat or man can be involved. Obviously, the dog gets infected when grooming itself, and humans, particularly children, can do the same. To control this worm, skin parasites as well as the worms must be controlled. Panacur will not remove this worm.

TAENIA: These are the very long tapeworms – some more than six feet! They have many mammalian hosts, but most commonly small rodents. So it is a risk in hunting dogs who eat their prey, or dogs fed shot rabbits.

ECHINOCCUS GRANULOSUS: This is a very short tapeworm, less than three inches. But it is the worm which produces the bladder worm on internal organs, usually the liver of animals who eat the excreted segments. The bladderworm is most common in sheep, but can produce illness in humans. Dogs working with sheep, or fed raw offal, should be regularly wormed to control human infection. Six-monthly multiwormer treatment, together with regular grooming and disposal of faeces is necessary to keep tapeworm infestation under control. Finally, when worming, dose all dogs on the premises at the same time, worm all new dogs on arrival, and worm new bitches with Fenbendazole.

HYDATID TAPEWORM: This parasite is found in many countries. It is particularly prevalent in New Zealand and Australia. Although it can infect humans the number is very small, but it can cause quite serious illness. People can only catch the disease from infected dogs. If dogs are regularly wormed and never allowed to eat raw meat, especially offal, there should not be any problems.

ALL ROUND WORMER

Bayer Animal Health of Tingalpa Australia have produced a wormer called Drontal, which they claim is safe and effective. With correct usage it is able to control Hookworms, Whipworms, Tapeworms and Roundworms. This should be of great help to Australian breeders and owners.

LYME DISEASE

Lyme disease is a chronic, multisystemic inflammatory disorder of man and animals, associated with infection by the tick-borne spirochaete, Borrelia burgdorferi. Ticks of the genus Ixodes are the most important vectors, and in Europe it is often associated with sheep and deer ticks.

It first appeared on the scene in Lyme, Connecticut, USA in 1975, and spread rapidly to most of North America. As far as is known, it was first reported in a dog in the UK in 1990, and has also been reported in several other European countries. Recently there has been a spate of scare stories in the Canine Press, and we have therefore asked Dr Christopher May of Liverpool University, to explain the situation more fully. Dr May has been doing research into Lyme disease, and his assessment of the situation in the UK is as follows:

"Lyme disease undoubtedly exists in UK dogs, but, at the present time, we believe that it is an uncommon problem. There are apparent 'hotspots' in the UK – the New Forest and Thetford area being two of them. However, dogs exposed to ticks almost anywhere in the UK, can be exposed to the causative organism of Lyme disease, which is Borrelia burgdorferi. In our survey approximately fifteen to twenty per cent of dogs exposed to ticks also had evidence that they were exposed to Borrelia burgdorferi. In spite of this, we have diagnosed clinical Lyme Disease in only a handful of dogs. Dogs presenting with Lyme disease usually have a fever; they may have enlarged lymph nodes and, in most cases, their main clinical feature will be lameness in one or more limbs. This is associated with inflammation as a result of Borrelia burgdorferi entering the joints. The lameness may occur weeks, or even months, after exposure to a tick, and does not occur at the same time as the tick bite. Sometimes, early in the disease, soon after the tick bite, the dog will suffer a non-specific illness, with fever and depression.

"Treatment requires antibiotics, which can only be prescribed by a veterinary surgeon after examining the dog concerned. Anyone who suspects their dog has Lyme Disease should contact their vet and arrange for the animal to be examined. In most cases, therapy is very successful."

Lyme disease is more of a problem in the US than in the UK. It is said to have tripled in humans since 1985, and it is expected that it will soon be a problem in all forty-eight contiguous States. Problems in domestic animals, including dogs, may be ten times the level found in humans. Dr Edward Baker VMD, a veterinarian at the Animal Skin and Allergy Clinic in Demarest considers that there is a tendency for the public to panic, but suggests some preventative measures which could help.

He recommends that if a dog has been exposed to a tick-infested environment, the dog should be thoroughly checked on returning home. Any ticks found should be carefully removed with tweezers, making sure that the whole head and mouthpiece are removed completely. Wash the bite with antiseptic. If it is suspected that the tick is a carrier, take it along to your vet for identification.

Once a tick is attached to the skin it can take anywhere from twelve to seventy-two hours for the spirochaete to be pumped into the new host; so if promptly removed, the danger of transmission is considerably reduced. Some insect repellants and flea collars can prove useful, but it is best to obtain professional advice on this. In 1990 Fort Lodge Laboratories brought out the first-ever vaccine to protect dogs against Lyme disease. This proved safe and effective, with a duration of immunity that lasts throughout the longest tick season.

FIRST AID

First aid is essentially emergency treatment to help the casualty to be made safe and comfortable until skilled help can be obtained. A knowledge of First aid should ensure that you do not panic when an emergency occurs.

DROWNING

Although most dogs can swim, accidents can, and do happen. Puppies can easily fall into fish ponds. Dogs can find they are unable to climb out of swimming pools, or an overhanging embankment. Having got the dog out of the water, lift by the back legs (if possible) and let the dog swing to allow the water to drain from the lungs. Place the dog on the ground on its right side, and check the breathing. If the dog is unconscious begin artificial respiration, or mouth to mouth resuscitation. If using the latter method, make sure the dog's mouth is shut, and force air in through the nose.

POISONING

If your dog has swallowed poison, and you know what it was, call your vet for advice. Wipe away any poison round the dog's mouth, or from the skin with warm water. If you can get your dog to vomit, and the vet recommends this course of action, do so. But not if the dog is having convulsions. If you suspect poisoning, but have no idea what the dog has taken, go straight to the vet.

BURNS

In all cases, apply cold water immediately, and keep applying it for ten or fifteen minutes. If your dog, or more likely a puppy, has chewed an electric wire, *switch off the current first*. Do not put anything on the burn, but take the dog straight to the vet.

HEAT STROKE

Dogs do not suffer from heat stroke only in hot climates; they are just as likely to suffer in any climate, especially if left in parked cars with little ventilation, and in the sun. In comparatively warm weather the temperature in a closed car can rise rapidly to 38C, so never leave your dog shut in a closed car. A dog suffering from heat stroke will show some, or all, of the following signs: panting, increased pulse rate, reddened eyes and gums, and probably vomiting. Take the dog to a cool, airy place and treat immediately by dousing with cold water. Once recovery is underway, dry your dog. Make sure your dog stays in the cool, and encourage him to drink. Then go straight to the vet .

CHOKING

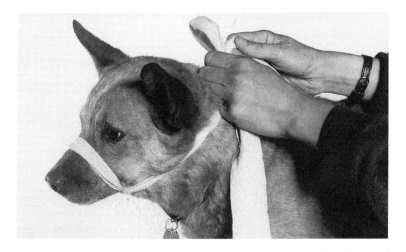

Putting on an emergency muzzle.

Sally Anne Thompson.

One of the commonest causes of choking is a small rubber ball, which can become jammed in the throat. Never try to push it, or any other object, down the throat. You could try laying the dog on its side and giving a sharp, strong downward push, just behind the last rib. If you have an assistant, get them to open the dog's mouth, and try to reach the ball, or whatever, as it is forced up.

Dogs can also get sticks wedged in their mouths, and they will get in a right panic about it. A dog in this situation will usually paw at the mouth, rush about dribbling and putting his head on the ground, scrabbling wildly. Try to find someone to help, and hold the dog firmly. Open the mouth and, if you can, wedge it open, otherwise you could easily get bitten. Then try to lever the foreign body out, making sure you have got it all.

TRAFFIC ACCIDENTS

If your dog is involved in a traffic accident – *do not panic*. The dog probably will, so it is up to you to remain calm and assess the situation. If not badly injured, most dogs hit by a car will instinctively try to run from the scene, so first try to restrain your dog. If badly injured, the dog will be scared and in shock, and will probably try to bite – yes, even the owner. So, unless the dog's head is injured, the first thing to do is to put on an emergency muzzle. Use anything available, such as a scarf, a large handkerchief, soft belt, bandage etc. Make a loop and slip it over the dog's nose, pull it tight under the chin, take it behind the ears and tie firmly.

If your dog is showing signs of shock – rapid, shallow breathing, clammy lips and gums, cold paws and ears, rapid heartbeat etc. – try to keep the dog warm and quiet. If there is a lot of blood from an obvious wound, apply a pressure bandage, using any clean material handy. Do not remove this if blood seeps through, bandage firmly on top. If there is a foreign object in the wound, you can probably safely remove it if it is small; but if it is a large object, leave it where it is until you can get the dog to the vet, having first bandaged round it. If the dog has internal injuries, these will not be obvious, except that the dog will be showing signs of shock. The best way to move an injured dog is on a makeshift stretcher, or on a car rug, if nothing else is available. Slide the rug, or a board if available, under the dog; do not lift the dog on to it. Enlist help so that someone can lift each end, and carefully carry the dog to the car. Make sure you get the dog to the vet as quickly as possible. If the dog is unconscious, check that its airways are clear, check for a heartbeat, and rush the dog to the vet.

Chapter Ten

SHOWING YOUR ACD

There are those who maintain that a good judge should be able to see the good and bad points of a dog, irrespective of presentation. What rubbish! Any animal from a fancy mouse to a shire horse depends on presentation to catch the judge's eye. Why do people try to look their best when they go for a job interview, or on a date with a member of the opposite sex?

Novice exhibitors often fail to realise that we were all novices once. When John started showing dogs sixty years ago, there were fewer opportunities to learn than are available now. There were few books, and no seminars, workshops, training classes and the like, which are readily available nowadays. In those days you had to learn by watching the experts, and that is still a good starting point for the novice.

Go to some shows and see what goes on. If it is your first dog show you are likely to be somewhat bewildered; but in time, all should become clear. There is a huge range of dog shows from vast Championship shows to the smaller and more informal events. At the unbenched shows in the UK, dogs and handlers tend to wander around aimlessly between classes. In Australia, Canada, and the US everyone claims a patch where the dogs, including puppies, are kept in crates or pens, with the owners in attendance. It all appears very haphazard, but it creates a much more social and 'shop window' atmosphere.

JUDGING PROCEDURE
FIRST IMPRESSION
The judge usually starts with all the dogs lined up round the ring. Then, with dogs on the handlers' left, they all move round the ring anti-clockwise. It is always a good idea to get to the head of the line-up, especially if you have a free-moving dog. You can then make your own pace, avoiding the risk of getting behind a 'slug'. There is nothing more aggravating than having a really good-moving dog, and being unable to show how good the dog is.

Of course, there will be others with similar ideas, and some experienced handlers are very clever at getting the best place in the line-up. The next best place is at the end. If the one in front is too slow, you can hang back a bit and then catch up, giving your dog a chance to extend. Bear in mind that all the other dogs may not be as well-behaved as your dog. Keep an eye on other exhibits, and if one is showing any signs of aggression, keep as far away as possible.

When the dogs are moving round the ring – or gaiting as it is called in the US – the judge will be making a comparison between all the entries. If it is a big class, the judge may keep the dogs moving for some time. When John is judging, he finds that the dog which really catches his eye at this stage is very often, although not always, the ultimate winner. Other judges also agree with this, so do not get the idea that you are only walking round for the exercise. A judge cannot watch all the dogs all the time, but some exhibitors seem to think this can be done. They keep their dog keyed up right from the start, so that by the time it comes to the final decision, the poor creature is completely fed up. Most judges watch the dogs as they move along one side of the ring, which means your dog will not be in view while you move round the other three sides. This is when you can let your dog relax. You can then get your dog keyed up, with lots of praise and encouragement, as you move down the side that the judge is watching. However, keep an eye on the judge just in case he/she has an extra look at your dog, which may well be the case if your dog is the one that has already caught the attention.

INDIVIDUAL EXAMINATION

Once the judge has seen all the dogs moving round the ring, the steward will ask everyone to stop. Each dog is now asked to move forward for examination by the judge. For those left in the line, this is another opportunity to relax, for both dog and handler. We make our dogs lie down when waiting their turn; nothing tires a dog more than standing still. Left to their own devices, dogs with nothing better to do, usually lie down. If the judge should cast a quick glance at your dog, at least no faults will be visible when the dog is in that position!

MOVING YOUR DOG

Once the judge has completed the individual examination, you will be asked to move your dog, and the usual practice nowadays is to move in a triangle. You move from the judge to the right-hand corner of the ring, turn smartly and proceed along the far side, turn at the end, and go straight back to the judge. When you are going away and coming back, the judge is looking to see if the dog is moving straight. This can only be assessed if you move the dog in a straight line. It has been known for exhibitors to be so intent on looking at their dog, that they have walked into the spectators sitting by the ringside! Keep an eye on your dog by all means, but before you start off, look to see where you are going, and go straight there. Coming back, remember that it is your dog, not you, the judge is looking at, which means that the dog should move straight towards the judge.

When you are moving across the end of the ring, the judge will be able to see how your dog moves broadside on. In a big class, you may not have been able to show this off to advantage while moving round the ring; some judges do not move dogs round the ring anyhow. This is your opportunity to make up for this.

PRESENTATION

There are differences of opinion as to how a dog should be presented to the judge. It seems to be the general practice in the US and Australia to stack ACDs for examination by the judge, although this does not apply to all breeds. When 'stacking', the dog is placed in position by hand, each foot being placed in its exact spot. The dog wears a thin collar close up to the cheeks, and the head is held up by a taut lead, held above the dog's head. The ACD is then usually 'baited' with food, in order to make the dog prick his ears and look alert. The winning dogs really do stand like statues, and it is obvious that a great deal of training has taken place.

In the UK there is no general practice in showing. Very few ACD exhibitors attempt to stack their dogs, and those who do, fail to make a very good job of it. So far, no professional handlers have appeared in the ring with ACDs, as is the general practice in the US, and with some breeds in the UK. Some exhibitors teach their dogs to stand back on a slack lead, while others show the ACD food in the right hand, and hold the dog back with the lead in the left hand.

FINAL PLACING

When the individual examinations have been completed, the judge will have another look at the whole class, and make a short list. Some judges will move the dogs round the ring again and pick them while they are moving. Others leave them standing and go from one to the other to pick out their winners. How many are pulled in to the centre depends on the number of prizes on offer, which, in turn, usually depends on the number of entries. Most judges pull in one or two more than the number of prizes on offer; if there are five prizes, six or seven exhibits would be called in.

Do not get too excited if you are called in first at this stage – judging is not finished yet! The steward will now politely ask the other exhibitors to leave the ring. This will make much more room for the judge to have a better look at the remaining dogs, especially if it was a big class. Some judges ask for the dogs to be taken round again when the extra space will afford a much better opportunity for everyone to show off their dog's paces. The dogs will then be lined up again in the centre of the ring for the judge to make a final decision. It is now that the dog which has been allowed to relax periodically will have the edge over the one that has been incessantly prodded, cajoled and stuffed with food from the time it first entered the ring.

TRAINING FOR THE SHOW RING
THE ART OF MOVING YOUR DOG

Training for the show ring can be divided into moving and standing still, and we will deal with movement first. The Breed Standard states: "The action is true, free, supple and tireless." Action cannot be free unless the dog is free – on a slack lead. No dog can move freely when suspended on a tight lead so that the front feet scarcely touch the ground, or if the dog is dragging the handler along. Worst of all is the dog which pulls out sideways, making it impossible for the judge to tell whether or not the animal can move straight, either coming or going. It is unnatural for a dog to trot with head held high, and efforts to make a dog do so often result in the 'stiltiness' referred to in the Standard as a serious fault.

Your first task, therefore, is to teach your dog to move freely on a slack lead. All dogs should walk on a slack lead, and we are assuming that you have taught your dog to do so from puppyhood; or to put it another way, you have not allowed your dog to get into the habit of pulling. Next you should practise moving at the pace you will be required to move at in the ring – for your own sake as well as that of the dog! This means running with the dog, unless you have a bike or a horse available.

Dogs move their best at different paces, and you should try to find out the best pace for your dog. It is not always easy to tell how your ACD is moving when you are running with the dog, and advice from an experienced onlooker is usually worth having. This particularly applies to going from, and coming to the judge, when it is usually better to move at a slower pace.

POSING YOUR DOG

We never stack a dog, and the following advice is based on what we have read, or learnt from watching those who use this method. It is really a question of practice, rather than actual training. The puppy is gradually accustomed to having a collar held tight round the throat, but the head is not pulled up into position by the lead. Instead, the head is pushed up by one hand, while the lead, held in the other hand, keeps the head in position.

The front feet are positioned by lifting the pup, with a hand under the chest, and putting the feet down firmly on the table. The hind feet are then placed in the correct position, one at a time, by hand. Once the puppy is in the correct position, reward with a treat, and then allow the pup to go and play. Needless to say, these sessions should be very short with a young puppy. We have been told that some breeders stack their promising show puppies every day. This seems a bit excessive, but provided the periods are short, it is certainly better than infrequent, lengthy sessions.

HANDLING IN THE RING

We never touch a dog of any breed in the show ring, other than giving a friendly pat when the dog has done well – or not done so well! The object of showing is to make the most of the dog's good points. We believe, rightly or wrongly, that the judge will see these more easily if the dog is standing four-square, well back from the handler. The spectators will also see the dog better in this position, and it is from this group that you will find prospective puppy buyers, stud dog users and other judges – sometimes better than the one in the ring!

When you have taught your ACD to stand on command, we have found that the best way to get that alert, all-attention look, is to teach the dog to catch food thrown by the handler. Some dogs are better at this than others, but all our ACDs have soon become experts. Having taught the dog to catch and stand on command, all that is necessary is to practise standing in the correct position. With a tidbit in the right hand, move your dog forward until the desired position is achieved, and then command "Stand" and "Stay". As soon as your dog is standing correctly, throw the food.

Once your ACD learns to catch food, you will find that the dog soon learns to watch the hand in anticipation of food being there, so there is no need to throw food round the ring, as some exhibitors do. Just throw the occasional bit at the end of the class, to keep the dog's interest. It is easy to persuade your dog to look in any direction, if the dog concentrates on watching your hand.

When the judge wants to see the dog's front, you can move to one side while the dog looks straight forward, as you hold your hand to the front. You can then move back while the judge looks at the other profile. To improve on all this, a dog can easily be taught to stand up from the down (see Chapter Eight). As already mentioned, we make a dog lie down when the judge is looking at the other dogs. If, as a judge approaches, your dog stands up to attention and says "Hey, look at me", it is most impressive and goes down well with the ringside.

CHOOSING YOUR STYLE OF HANDLING

We do not expect all our readers to agree with our method of showing – nor would we want them to suddenly change from their own method. The well-known American trainer/behaviourist, Gail Fisher, says that in her part of the US there is a saying "If it ain't broke, don't fix it." If you are having success with your own method, and particularly if your dog has been trained in that way, it would be very unwise to suddenly change.

However, to those with an open mind, we would suggest they look at a lot of photographs of ACDs, and decide for themselves which present the best pictures – those suspended on a tight lead, or those standing on a loose lead, or with no lead at all. Some say the object of having the collar as high up the neck as possible is to make the neck look longer. But the same effect can be obtained by having it as low down the neck as possible, as is the fashion in quite a few breeds. In any case, the neck should be "of medium length broadening to blend into the body" – not as long as possible and coming out of the body at a right angle.

THE IMPORTANCE Of 'GOOD' TEMPERAMENT

Whatever method of showing you intend to use, it is absolutely essential that your dog is amenable to handling. If properly brought up, your dog will be quite happy for you to make an intimate examination: to look at the mouth, handle the body, pick up the feet, handle the tail, not forgetting

CHOOSING YOUR STLYE OF HANDLING

Formakin Minkie on a tight lead.
Sally Anne Thompson.

The same dog on a slack lead.
Sally Anne Thompson

A double-action slip collar, correctly fitted.

Sally Anne Thompson

that a male must have the testicles handled. But while most dogs with good temperaments are quite happy for the owner to do all this, a lot of ACDs do not care for a stranger doing it – and certainly they would object to those judges who maul dogs, rather than handle them. Training classes, particularly those specialising in ring training, are a great help in this direction, as are any gatherings of dog fanciers who will help by pretending to be judges.

SHOW PREPARATION
A few days before a show, give your ACD a thorough grooming to get rid of any loose or dead hair. Clean your dog's ears and teeth, and check that the nails are short. If you need to use nail clippers, you will get a better finish if you go over the nails with a file afterwards. Follow this by a good bath; dry your dog, and make sure that you brush the coat down so that it lies flat.

   To save time and panic on the morning of the show, try to have everything ready the night before. If you are rushing around, grabbing this and that and yelling at the family, you will only get the dog upset, which is the last thing you want to do before a show. The equipment you require is:

A bowl.
A bottle of water.
A brush.
A comb.
A soft cloth.
A towel (maybe two, if it looks like rain!).
A strong-buckled collar.
Bench chain (if the show is benched) or crate.
Travelling crate (if this is your dog's usual mode of transport).
Show collar and lead.

Never show your dog on a thick collar with a piece of rope attached – yes, some people do just that! You are trying to make the dog look his best, so have a neat, narrow, but strong collar and lead which will complement your dog's appearance. We use a double action, small link, chain collar which, if properly fitted, can be slackened off to lie down on the shoulders, showing off the dog's neck to advantage. But so long as it is neat, it is up to you to use whatever type you prefer.

FEEDING
We never feed our ACDs before going to a show, unless it is going to be a very long journey, when a light meal is allowed. We do not feed at the show, but we often take along some milk and honey. A drink of milk with a spoonful of honey tops up the energy requirements without filling the dog up. One thing not to forget is tidbits; these will be a great help when showing. We find that liver treats, either bought ones, or homemade by baking some liver and chopping it up small, are best. Nearly all dogs love liver, and if you keep it as a special treat for show days, you will get that little bit extra out of your dog in the show ring.

AT THE SHOW
When you arrive at the show, take the dog to the exercise area to 'empty'. Just as important, take along a plastic bag and pick up after your dog. Go to your allocated bench, or wherever you have 'set up camp', and give your dog a good brush over. Just before your class is due, wipe your dog all over with a damp cloth to remove any loose hairs; give a final polish with a soft cloth, put on the show collar and lead, and you are ready for the fray. If there has been a long wait before the class, make sure the dog has a chance to 'empty' again.

Never go to a show if your dog is the slightest bit off-colour, or out of coat. Dogs shows are great places for picking up infections, and a dog slightly under the weather is prey to any and every nasty bug that might be going around. A dog show is a beauty contest and a dog out of coat can never look his best. It is an insult to both dog and judge to show a dog in that condition. You would not be doing yourself a favour either, and the ringside will certainly not be impressed with your pride and joy. Dog shows are meant to be fun for you and your dog, so don't take it all too seriously. If you win, it is a bonus. But win or lose, you still have the same dog, who is your best friend – and there will always be another day.

Chapter Eleven

THE WORKING ACD

DEVELOPMENT OF THE WORKING DOG

There seems to be little doubt that the reason why early man first domesticated the dog was because of its hunting instinct. The wolf cub, taken from the nest, would one day help its owner catch food. In quite recent times (perhaps even today) the Australian Aborigines took Dingo pups from the nest, reared them with the family and used them for hunting. By breeding from the best hunters, man produced dogs which hunted even better. It is because of this that many of today's dogs have a much stronger hunting instinct than their wild ancestry. While the wild dog hunts when it is hungry, there are many domestic dogs which hunt the uneatable, and keep on hunting just for fun.

When man started farming and domesticating other animals, it would be natural to use dogs to help in the control of grazing stock. By careful selective breeding, the hunting instinct was adapted to produce other instincts; as far as we are concerned, the most important of these is the herding instinct. When a pack of wild dogs is hunting, one or two of the faster ones often head the quarry and turn it back to the slower ones coming up behind. By breeding from such dogs, it is quite possible that strains and breeds would have been produced which would instinctively head stock and turn it back to the "pack leader". At least, that is how we imagine the development of many herding breeds, which have proved invaluable to man through the ages.

THE ACD AS A DRIVING BREED

There are, of course, those who say that the ACD is a driving breed, which should work between the stock and handler, and should never ever head. There are also those who disagree with that, and some, who at least have doubts. John has had letters from novices in the US asking for his opinion on this subject. It appears that some instructors at stock dog clinics will not allow dogs of what they regard as driving breeds, to head stock under any circumstances. This means that in the confines of the training arena the dog just pushes the stock along from behind, while the handler turns it in the direction required.

There is no need for a specially bred dog to do that. When John was a boy, he had a terrier, of sorts, which could have matched any ACD at heeling cattle. But if the cattle went the wrong way, he just drove them all the faster! John also had a Cairn Terrier which was great at forcing sheep into pens, or through muddy gateways, and she would go over their backs too! More recently, we had a Labrador-Golden Retriever cross, who would drive either cattle or sheep by barking at them. And just to prove that ACDs are by no means the only breed with a herding instinct, the most persistent heeler of horses we ever had was a Pekingese!

That should be sufficient evidence to prove that nearly any dog with initiative can be trained to drive stock. But one of our main reasons for keeping a dog is in the hope that it will do things we cannot do, and sometimes things we do not want to do. One of the things we cannot do is run fast enough to pass a steer which has broken away from the others. A good heading dog will be after it and turn it back, before even being told to do so. Another task we never cared for was running round a field, early in the morning darkness, gathering a herd of cows for milking. We liked to be able to open the gate, send the dog, and return to the yard to await the arrival of the cows, with the dog behind them. A driving dog would be a help, but someone would have to stay with the dog, behind the cows.

It is true to say that most ACDs prefer driving to fetching, and many appear to be devoid of any true herding instinct. However, that has not always been the case. In *Barkers and Biters*, Kaleski writes: "The best time to see his value is when the cattle try to get away from the drover – whether at an awkward corner in broken country or through scrub or crowded streets. Then as the leaders swing away – with the whole mob to follow if they are successful – the drover whistles; like an arrow his dog shoots up to those leaders. Snap! Snap! at the throat of the one he wants to turn, and it swings him as on a pivot, jambing the other leader over as well. Nip! Nip! at their heels; and they dart along the right track, followed by those behind, while the dog stands watching at the weak point till all are past. No human being could work like that; the cattle would be tearing down the wrong track, unheadable, before he would be halfway to them.

"Or again: a dark, drizzling night, with the drover pushing on to reach his favourite camp or deliver the cattle. He rides ahead of the mob, trusting to instinct, the night is black as the Pit. Behind him follow the cattle; unwillingly but forced forward by the determined watcher behind. As the rogues fall back, in hopes of standing till the mob has passed, they receive a series of heelnips which make them bellow again and dart into the mob for shelter. There may be a thousand head behind the drover; but never a one will be missing at the sliprails, thanks to the cattle dog."

Exciting stuff, which certainly doesn't suggest that the early breeders intended the ACD to be purely a driving dog. The late Scott Lithgow, famous breeder and trainer of cattle dogs in Queensland, sent us a copy of his excellent book, *Training and Working Dogs: For Quiet, Confident Control of Stock*. He writes, with special emphasis: "No dog can effectively control cattle if he will not head." While expressing a great weakness for the 'Queensland Heeler', he laments the increasing difficulty in finding any that will head, or are indeed physically capable of working at all.

PRESENT-DAY WORKING CAPABILITIES

To try to find out more about working cattle dogs in Australia, we contacted Scott Lithgow's son Kent, and have also had several discussions with Pete Thompson, a friend of the Lithgows. They both share Scott's views about the type of ACD being bred for the show ring, a view shared by B. Southall of Queensland. He has written an article published in the *Queensland Dog World* of August 1992, headed "What have we done to the Australian Cattle Dog?" Southall both works and shows ACDs, and he writes:

"The only way I can breed the dogs so I can have some show dogs and some workers is to breed two different types." He maintains that the ACDs winning in the show ring in Australia are too short in leg, too heavy in bone, loaded in shoulder and coarse in head – "he has to carry it around all day." These are the views of men who depend on dogs to work cattle in Queensland, birthplace of the breed.

John finds this particularly worrying, in relation to his experience with Corgis. When he started breeding Corgis in 1933, the Pembrokes and Cardigans were still one breed. John bred Pembrokes and worked them regularly on cattle, but they had legs and were amazingly athletic. It is probable that some of today's show ring Corgis have retained the working instinct, but they are physically incapable of using it. The Corgi is still a nice little dog, but it could still have been a nice little dog, with legs, if judges had not interpreted "ample bone" as "most bone" and "legs short" as "shortest legs".

Many parts of the Australian outback are covered by dense scrub, impenetrable to a man on horseback. And the modern cowboys in their helicopters cannot get cattle out of these areas either. But dogs can, provided they will get round behind the cattle and bring them out to the drovers. Because so few ACDs will do this, they have been crossed with Border Collies and Kelpies to produce dogs which will cast out and gather, while still retaining the toughness of the 'Heeler'. ACDs are still used for forcing big mobs of cattle, but they work with heading dogs that turn back any which break away. John's Corgis worked on very much the same principle, but, of course, on a much smaller scale. A Corgi is neither fast enough, nor strong enough, to turn a runaway steer. But because the Corgi bites so low in the soft part of the heel, the breed can drive cattle just as effectively as an ACD. John always worked his Corgis with a Collie that would head – which is not much help to those who want to keep only one dog. The ACD is quite capable of heading, though some are not very willing to do so.

WORKING TRIALS
Working Trials for cattle dogs are popular in Australia, but because the ACD cannot cope with the tests involved, they never take part. Bearing in mind the many breeds which work cattle worldwide, we have always regretted that the old title of 'Queensland Heeler' was not adhered to. It would certainly have avoided having cattle dog trials in Australia, with no Australian Cattle Dogs!

In the US and Canada the situation is very different, with stock dogs trials and clinics for every conceivable herding breed of dog. John was a guest of the Australian Cattle Dog Club of America at its National Convention in Tulsa in 1988, and there he saw cattle dog trials and learnt a lot about the ACDs and their owners. He was pleased to see that most of the dogs taking part in the Working Trials were also show dogs. Indeed, several dogs were winning one day in the herding arena and next day in the show ring. Admittedly, these trials – or any trials, for that matter – do not provide an accurate picture of a dog's working ability under practical conditions. But they do prove that the dog will work. They also provide an opportunity for breeders and judges to see dogs working – and how many of our famous all rounders, who judge dogs worldwide, have ever seen a dog working cattle?

Since then the American Kennel Club has granted working qualifications for stock dogs. Kent and Lori Herbel, successful breeders, exhibitors and trainers of ACDs in the US, have travelled all over America, under the auspices of the AKC, helping with the new Herding Program, and much of its success is due to their efforts. They also organise and instruct at many stock dog training clinics. They provide the following insight into working ACDs in the US.

HERDING IN THE UNITED STATES
By Kent and Lori Herbel
The Australian Cattle Dog is today the most common AKC herding breed used on American ranches. Often referred to by the common nicknames of 'Blue Heeler' or 'Queensland Heeler',

most of these stockdogs are purebred Australian Cattle Dogs. Cattle ranchers in the US, especially value the help of an Australian Cattle Dog because this breed excels at exactly what it was developed for in the Australian outback ... truly a droving dog built to withstand many miles and long days, agile enough to keep up with a horse and intelligent enough to handle cattle in an efficient way. Additionally, many American ranchers use alleys and chutes when working or loading cattle. The Australian Cattle Dog is invaluable in moving cattle single file through this equipment by darting under fences, gripping heels and ducking out. Though the days of long cattle drives to market are gone, many ranchers still move their cattle from pasture to pasture, or gather cattle each spring or fall. A well-trained Australian Cattle Dog can take the place of several men whether helping with daily chores or the annual round-up.

In addition to exhibiting their talent on the ranch, Australian Cattle Dogs are quite popular in herding competition. Herding as a sport is becoming quite popular throughout the United States as many breeders and owners are realizing the importance of preserving the origins and heritage of the herding dogs. There are various herding programs in which Australian Cattle Dogs are eligible to compete, including the American Kennel Club (AKC), Australian Shepherd Club of America (ASCA), American Herding Breeds Association (AHBA), and various Border Collie organizations, which usually follow the rules of the International Sheep Dog Society.

The Australian Cattle Dog Club of America (ACDCA) began their own herding program in 1978 when club members saw the need to promote the preservation of herding instinct. A Versatility Program was carefully developed, with emphasis not only on working instinct, but also stressing trainability through Obedience as well as the importance of conformation. Dogs were required to qualify in each category before being eligible to earn the title VQW (Versatility Qualified Worker). Each category (Working, Obedience and Conformation) was worth 100 points. Competing dogs were not only required to get at least 50 points in each category, but were also required to have an overall score of at least 200 points in the regular class, or 250 points at the Advanced level, to qualify.

Conformation points were based on height, overall conformation, head and neck, gait and movement, feet, color and coat. In Obedience, dogs were required to work off leash, with points reflecting their work on Heeling, Recall, Sit for exam, and Stay for one minute. The Working section called for the dogs to work five head of stock through a pre-determined course, which varied from year to year. Categories scored included response to handler, biting style, herding style, herding ability, and number of cattle penned at the end of the run. A Working Only trial was also available, and qualifying dogs had to earn at least 75 points. This title was designated as Qualified Worker (QW).

The American Kennel Club herding program went into effect in January of 1990. The ACDCA adopted this program to replace the Versatility program. Australian Cattle Dog owners were excited at the opportunity to earn herding titles, which would be AKC recognized and displayed on their AKC registration papers. The ACDCA took a strong stand in supporting the American Kennel Club herding program, and because of their experience with the Versatility Program, were given the privilege of hosting the first AKC trials. These trials were held on January 6th and 7th, 1990 at the Tulsa State Fairgrounds in Tulsa, Oklahoma, and were judged by Roger Beers of Luverne, Minnesota, a long-time, well-known Australian Cattle Dog breeder, and Robert Carrillo of Sebastopol, California, an Australian Kelpie breeder with an extensive background in herding. Attending this historic event were many members and officers of the ACDCA, and AKC representative Roberta Campbell, Administrator of Performance Events.

Placing High in Trial at the first AKC trial was a red dog, Cattlenip Red Collarenebri, bred and

Cattlenip Red Collarenbri (Am. Can. Ch. Turrella Red Rusty – Cattlenip Block N Tackle): first AKC High in Trial winner, Bred by Dawn O'Reilly, owned by Kent and Lori Herbel.

Lori Herbel.

shown by Dawn O'Reilly of Alberta, Canada, with a score of 89 in the Started Class. Reserve High in Trial went to Ch. Buzzard's Rope to Catchem, a blue dog, owned by Cappy and Pam Pruett of Ponca City, Oklahoma. The second day of events was won by a veteran red dog, eleven-year-old Ch. Buzzards Red Tubs, owned by Jim Buzzard of Vinita, Oklahoma, with a High in Trial score of 93 points. Reserve High in Trial went to Holly Wood Utley, UD, a blue female, owned by Terri Shoup of Catoosa, Oklahoma. Dogs competing in the weekend of events were from Florida, Oklahoma, Montana, Colorado and Canada.

In May of 1990, the ACDCA held a second weekend of licensed AKC Herding Trials in Tulsa. This time a sanctioned Herding Test was added for those handlers who felt their dogs were not quite ready to compete at the trialing level. Australian Cattle Dogs again made history as Ch. Buzzards Red Tubs was the first dog of any breed to earn the AKC Herding Excellent title; Ch. Jambo Kings Welah, and Jambo LDT's Troubadour, both owned by Tony and Betty Maeder, and Ch. Buzzards Rope to Catchem were among the first dogs of all herding breeds to complete the requirements for Herding Started titles.

THE AMERICAN KENNEL CLUB HERDING PROGRAM

All dogs, at least nine months of age, who are registered as a herding breed with the American Kennel Club, are eligible to compete in AKC herding tests and trials. All herding events are judged by approved AKC judges, who must have an extensive background in herding with experience in training and working stockdogs. Stock used may include ducks, sheep, goats or cattle.

The AKC program consists of three levels of competition: Herding Tested, Pre-Trial Testing, and Herding Trials. In addition, when a dog has earned the Advanced level trialing title, he may then continue competing for a Herding Championship, designated by an H.Ch. preceding his name. To earn this highest title, a dog must accumulate 15 Championship points by defeating other Advanced dogs. At least two major wins are also required, under two different judges.

HERDING TEST

Time allowed: 10 minutes
Arena size: Sheep and Cattle Minimum 100 feet x 100 feet
Maximum 100 feet x 200 feet
Ducks   50 feet x 100 feet
Round corners on all herding test arenas

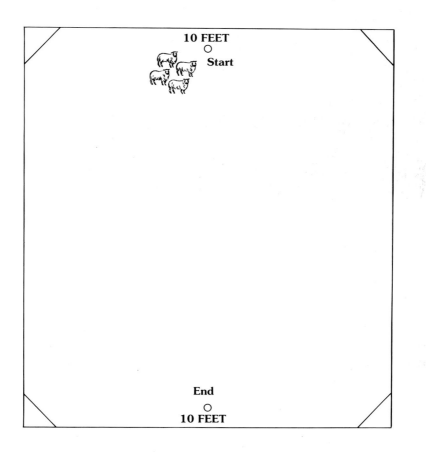

HERDING TEST: The first level is relatively simple, with dogs required to exhibit controlled movement of stock, as well as responsiveness to the handler. A small (100ft by 100ft) pen is used, with three to five head of stock. The dog must exhibit the following elements to pass the test: a stay at the beginning of the test, two controlled changes of direction of the stock, a stop, followed by a recall. The dog is allowed ten minutes in which to show the judge these exercises. At this level, dogs are simply judged whether they pass or fail, and no score is given. Two qualifying runs are required from two different judges in order for a dog to earn the Herding Tested title, designated by the letters 'HT' following his name.

PRE-TRIAL TEST

Time allowed: 10 minutes
Arena size: Sheep and Cattle Minimum 100 feet x 100 feet
Maximum 200 feet x 400 feet
Ducks **50 feet x 100 feet**

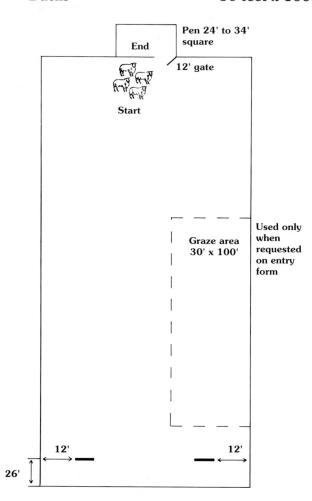

PRE-TRIAL TEST: The next level of competition, Pre-Trial Tested, is the dog's first introduction to working stock through obstacles. This test is held in an arena approximately 100ft by 200ft. A 'J'-shaped course is run, with the dog moving the stock down the arena wall and through two sets of panels, where they must then stop the stock, turn them and reverse the course. The run is completed when the dog pens the stock within the ten minute time limit. This level is also pass or fail, with no score given. The dog must pass this test under two different judges to earn the Pre-Trial Tested title (PT).

Kuawarri Munya Beron (George – Buzzards Katie May) working sheep through the centre panels on the Started A Course. Owned by Larry Painter, handled by Casey Painter of Belton Missouri.   *Lori Herbel.*

HERDING TRIAL: Dogs trained at the trialing level may exhibit their skills in their choice of three courses, 'A', 'B', or 'C'. Each course is designed to showcase a different style of working. Individual dogs are not required to work in a particular manner according to breed characteristics. Dogs may drive or fetch or may combine both working styles in order to complete the courses. Three levels of competition on each course are offered: Herding Started (HS), Herding Intermediate (HI), and Advanced, which earns the Herding Excellent (HX) title. At each of these levels, three qualifying scores under three different judges are required.

A qualifying score at the trialing level requires the dog to earn at least 60 out of 100 possible points, which are derived from six categories. In addition, a dog must earn at least half of the points in each individual category.

'A' COURSE

The 'A' Course is the course which has been used at the Australian Cattle Dog Club of America National Specialties since 1989. It is a farm/ranch course held in an arena approximately 100ft by 200ft, designed to simulate actual ranch situations, such as chutes, gates and examining pens. Again, a ten minute time limit is set, and the dog is required to move the stock through the obstacles in a specific order. Points may be deducted for unnecessary biting, splitting stock, losing control of the stock, retreating on course, lack of interest, etc.

At the **Started** level, a dog may have some assistance by the handler, who is allowed to walk through the course with the dog. The Started dog begins with the stock at one end of the arena. The first obstacle is a Y-shaped chute halfway down the arena wall, followed by a 90-degree turn at the opposite end of the arena and into a Z-shaped chute along the wall. The dog must then take the stock directly to the corner of the arena, where they must turn and head straight through a Panel Run-Way. Approximately two-thirds of the way back up the arena, the dog must direct the stock back across the middle of the arena through two Center Line Panels. Taking the stock directly to the arena wall, the dog should then hold the stock in this area until the handler can open the pen. The run is completed when all the stock are penned and the gate is closed.

The next level of trialing is **Intermediate,** which requires more of the work to be done by the dog with less assistance from the handler. A small outrun is introduced at this level, requiring the

COURSE A: STARTED

Time allowed: 10 minutes
Arena size: Sheep and Cattle Minimum 100 feet x 100 feet
                          Maximum 200 feet x 400 feet
           Ducks   Minimum   50 feet x 100 feet
                          Maximum 100 feet x 200 feet

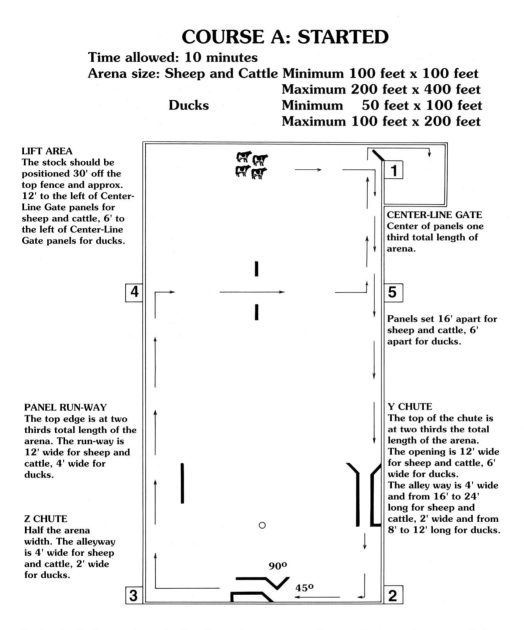

LIFT AREA
The stock should be positioned 30' off the top fence and approx. 12' to the left of Center-Line Gate panels for sheep and cattle, 6' to the left of Center-Line Gate panels for ducks.

CENTER-LINE GATE
Center of panels one third total length of arena.

Panels set 16' apart for sheep and cattle, 6' apart for ducks.

PANEL RUN-WAY
The top edge is at two thirds total length of the arena. The run-way is 12' wide for sheep and cattle, 4' wide for ducks.

Y CHUTE
The top of the chute is at two thirds the total length of the arena. The opening is 12' wide for sheep and cattle, 6' wide for ducks. The alley way is 4' wide and from 16' to 24' long for sheep and cattle, 2' wide and from 8' to 12' long for ducks.

Z CHUTE
Half the arena width. The alleyway is 4' wide for sheep and cattle, 2' wide for ducks.

dog to fetch the stock to the handler, who must remain at a designated post until the outrun, lift and fetch is completed. The handler is then allowed to walk directly to each obstacle during the run, but must direct the dog from a reasonable distance. While the Y and Z-shaped chutes remain the same as in Started, the Panel Run-Way is now a Hold/Exam pen, which is a three-sided pen where the dog must put the stock and hold them until the judge is satisfied that the dog has demonstrated proper control. The remainder of the course is the same as in Started.

Advanced level trialing requires the dog to move the stock through most of the course with only verbal help from the handler. A handler's post is designated near one end of the arena, and the dog

COURSE A: INTERMEDIATE

Time allowed: 10 minutes
Arena size: Sheep and Cattle Minimum 100 feet x 100 feet
Maximum 200 feet x 400 feet
Ducks   Minimum   50 feet x 100 feet
Maximum 100 feet x 200 feet

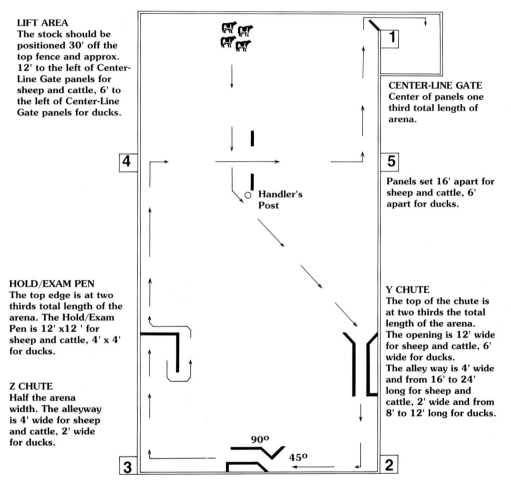

LIFT AREA
The stock should be positioned 30' off the top fence and approx. 12' to the left of Center-Line Gate panels for sheep and cattle, 6' to the left of Center-Line Gate panels for ducks.

CENTER-LINE GATE
Center of panels one third total length of arena.

Panels set 16' apart for sheep and cattle, 6' apart for ducks.

HOLD/EXAM PEN
The top edge is at two thirds total length of the arena. The Hold/Exam Pen is 12' x12 ' for sheep and cattle, 4' x 4' for ducks.

Z CHUTE
Half the arena width. The alleyway is 4' wide for sheep and cattle, 2' wide for ducks.

Y CHUTE
The top of the chute is at two thirds the total length of the arena. The opening is 12' wide for sheep and cattle, 6' wide for ducks. The alley way is 4' wide and from 16' to 24' long for sheep and cattle, 2' wide and from 8' to 12' long for ducks.

is sent on an outrun almost the full length of the arena. The dog should bring the stock in a direct line to the handler, take them in a half-circle around behind the handler and then progress on to the Y- and Z-shaped chutes. Only after these exercises are completed may the handler leave his post, and walk directly toward the Exam Pen. After completing the Exam Pen, the dog must take the stock out of the pen and complete a cross-drive through the Center Panels, and then hold the stock while the handler goes to the pen to open the gate. The dog pens the stock and the run is over. All levels on Course 'A' have a ten minute time limit.

More information on the AKC Herding Program can be obtained by writing to the American

COURSE A: ADVANCED

Time allowed: 10 minutes
Arena size: Sheep and Cattle Minimum 100 feet x 100 feet
Maximum 200 feet x 400 feet
Ducks   Minimum   50 feet x 100 feet
Maximum 100 feet x 200 feet

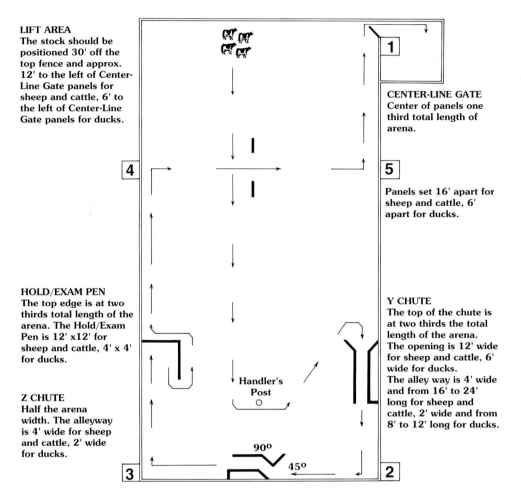

LIFT AREA
The stock should be positioned 30' off the top fence and approx. 12' to the left of Center-Line Gate panels for sheep and cattle, 6' to the left of Center-Line Gate panels for ducks.

1

CENTER-LINE GATE
Center of panels one third total length of arena.

4

5

Panels set 16' apart for sheep and cattle, 6' apart for ducks.

HOLD/EXAM PEN
The top edge is at two thirds total length of the arena. The Hold/Exam Pen is 12' x12' for sheep and cattle, 4' x 4' for ducks.

Y CHUTE
The top of the chute is at two thirds the total length of the arena. The opening is 12' wide for sheep and cattle, 6' wide for ducks. The alley way is 4' wide and from 16' to 24' long for sheep and cattle, 2' wide and from 8' to 12' long for ducks.

Z CHUTE
Half the arena width. The alleyway is 4' wide for sheep and cattle, 2' wide for ducks.

Handler's Post

90°

45°

3

2

Kennel Club, Herding Department, 51 Madison Avenue, New York, NY 10010. The AKC Herding Program Newsletter, *The Herdsman*, is a bi-monthly publication with training articles, event calendars, livestock handling articles, etc. For information contact Lori Herbel, Route 1 Box 52A, Putnam, OK 73659.

While Australian Cattle Dogs, with proper training, are capable of working on all courses, most seem to compete and excel on the 'A' Course. Although many have earned their titles on cattle, quite a few are now competing on sheep, and frequently work both types of stock during the same weekend.

Ch. Buzzards Bo of Whiskey River HX, VQW: driving cattle towards the Y chute at the Advanced level of Course A. The handler (Kent Herbel) must remain at the handler's post throughout most of the course.

Lori Herbel.

Penning the stock completes the course.

Lori Herbel.

To complement their herding program, the American Kennel Club also hosts educational Herding Clinics throughout the United States several times a year. Demonstrations at all levels of the program are scheduled, and Australian Cattle Dogs are quite often seen at these clinics using their talents. Judges, as well as exhibitors, sign up for these clinics to learn more about the judging and points system of the AKC program, and to learn about the characteristics and working styles of each breed.

Breed parent clubs, stockdog organizations and trainers throughout the US also hold herding clinics, sometimes in conjunction with tests, trials, and National Specialties. Handlers, owners,

Can. Ch. Cubaroo's Just A Two Bites, CDX, HS (Blue Pine Herdsman – Cubaroo's Pumkin B Mine) owned and handled by Kathy Eggleston, Antwerp, NY. High in Trial 1992 ACDCA National Specialty. Bred by Carrol Wells.
Lori Herbel.

breeders and trainers benefit from working with experienced instructors one-on-one with a dog on livestock. Participants can vary from dogs being exposed to livestock for first-time evaluation, to advanced level handlers working through problem areas, to handlers simply looking for new training techniques.

The Australian Cattle Dog has definitely made a place for itself as a top-notch herding dog in America. The popularity of the breed has grown in recent years as Australian Cattle Dog breeders have selected for correct temperament, instinct, structure and trainability. The Australian Cattle Dog in the United States is a working dog that can, indeed, go right from the ranch to the show ring or herding arena and win.

It is indeed pleasing that the AKC recognises the value of working stock dogs, but it is unfortunate that the same qualifications are awarded irrespective of the type of stock that is worked. There is nothing wrong with ACDs working sheep or ducks; this surely proves the versatility of the breed. However, we have known many excellent sheepdogs which would not face cattle under any circumstances. And ducks will move away from a dog just because it is there; all the dog has to do is move in the right direction. The AKC is unlikely to change its rules, so it is important that those who want a dog to work cattle should make sure they buy a puppy from dogs that work cattle, irrespective of what titles they have to their names.

We have only included particulars of Course 'A', which is the one used at the ACD Specialties. It is also the only one where cattle are used, although you can choose to work sheep or ducks if you wish. As this is a book about cattle dogs, I hope that most readers will want to work their dogs on cattle eventually, even if they start off with sheep.

TRAINING FOR WORK

As previously stated, it is the herding instinct which makes a dog want to work; but training, assisted to a greater or lesser degree by the submissive instinct, teaches the dog how to work. The snag is that it is impossible to tell by looking at a dog how strong the herding instinct is, or whether, in fact, there is any there at all. It is also impossible to tell the age at which the instinct is going to make an appearance in a particular puppy. All you can do is hope, and wait patiently until the puppy shows clearly that it wants to work.

The age at which this happens varies enormously. Some quite small puppies think they can take on a whole herd of cattle, and they have to be protected from their own instincts. Others take much longer. John once had a well-bred sheepdog pup, called Jed. At eight weeks old, Jed accompanied his mother and John on a daily round of the stock. Jed watched his mother working, but never showed the slightest inclination to follow her, and he paid no attention to the sheep, cattle or poultry in the yard. Jed grew into a handsome dog, obedient and affectionate, and no trouble at all, which is probably why he was kept on.

One day, when Jed was just over a year old, John went through a gate into a field where a flock of sheep were grazing. As he was closing the gate, Jed, quite suddenly, took off. John said nothing, but watched in amazement, as this young dog ran wide in a nice, easy lope, quietly gathered the whole flock and brought it right up to John. This was a much bigger flock in a much larger field than most young dogs could cope with. From that day, from that minute in fact, Jed was a very useful worker.

In an article in an ACDCA Newsletter on 'Starting a Young Cattle Dog', Betty Maeder writes: "If your pup is not showing the interest you want, or starting to work stock after several weeks or months of exposure, don't get discouraged. Most of you remember Jai, the dog Tony worked and trialed so successfully for several years; he never showed interest in stock until he was fifteen months old. He had always been right behind Tony, or sitting on the sidelines, or watching while the work was being done, then Bingo! A light seemed to go on, and he started working one day. It was as if he had been absorbing and evaluating everything he had seen for all those months. Before he was two, he was placing in trials."

So have patience and wait! This does not mean that the puppy will not be learning anything. In fact, puppies which do not 'start to run' until later, are often easier to train than those which start early. The better education they have had – or should have had – the easier it will be to control the herding instinct.

STOP ON COMMAND

By far the most important exercise is the stop command. It is the only absolutely essential exercise which a dog must understand before being allowed to work. It is very useful if the dog will come to you when called. But if the dog lies down and stays there, you can go up and attach a lead, as we have frequently done with young Border Collies with over-developed herding instincts. It is not essential that the dog lies down, so long as the dog stops and does not move until told to do so.

John teaches dogs to lie down, as he has found it easier to teach a dog to stay on the Down, than on either the Stand or the Sit. However, he likes a dog to stand when working, and this is encouraged, as soon as the dog is steady. A dog that stays on his feet can usually steady stock better than one that is bobbing up and down all the time.

DEVELOPMENT OF THE WORKING INSTINCT

In most puppies the working instinct develops gradually, the puppy becoming more and more interested in stock. Much as this is to be desired, it can give rise to problems. A young puppy who wants to work can easily be injured; a youngster can be kicked or trodden on by a cow or horse, or

Formakin Kulta working sheep in the UK. Working cattle excites an ACD more than working sheep, so it is a good idea to start a youngster on sheep.

Sally Anne Thompson.

attacked by an aggressive sheep – even a broody hen with chicks can be a formidable enemy to an unsuspecting puppy. Any of these experiences is likely to have one of two results, depending on the temperament of the puppy. At the one extreme, the puppy could be frightened, and is put off working. At the other extreme, it could encourage an aggressive puppy to attack and possibly kill the adversary.

The other problem which can arise is when the puppy is punished much too severely for a 'crime' which is due to the working instinct. A puppy must not be allowed to kill your pet lamb, but neither should the pup think that the lamb is 'out of bounds'. Too much strict obedience can inhibit a puppy's herding instinct. That instinct tells a dog to herd, but the submissive instinct tells a dog that the 'boss' might not approve. It then depends on whether the herding or the submissive instinct is the stronger.

Even if willing, an ACD should not be allowed to work cattle until seven or eight months of age. A dog should then be strong enough to stand a kick, and also faster than the cattle that are being herded. If you intend starting your ACD on cattle, it is important that they are the right sort. Weaned calves or dairy cows, who are accustomed to a dog, are probably best, but they must have been trained by a good dog! Cattle that have been chased about by an uncontrollable dog are usually more difficult to handle than those which have never seen a dog.

Working cattle usually excites a dog more than working sheep, and so John prefers to start a youngster on sheep. Once your ACD is under control and understands the commands, then you can move on to cattle. Do not get the idea that working sheep will make a dog too 'soft' for cattle. If a dog has what it takes, that dog will work cattle, sheep or no sheep. If a dog has not got what it takes, you might as well forget it!

Some sheepdog trainers start their young dogs on ducks, and have done so for a long time. John has often used ducks, which have certain advantages when starting a young dog, over either sheep or cattle. Ducks will move away from a dog without any effort on the dog's part. All the dog has to do is move in the right direction, and the ducks will respond accordingly. This makes them ideal for teaching control, and to encourage a young dog to move in various directions on command.

Some people teach a young dog to know his 'sides' before proper work commences. This is usually done by mechanical means, like tying the youngster to the end of a pole and moving it from left to right. John is not keen on mixing mechanics with training, and he has never found it necessary. On the other hand, the more the dog understands before starting to work, the easier that dog will be to control.

COMMANDS

Ideally, a novice should start with a trained dog, but some do start from scratch and make a very good job of it. Some people have more trouble learning to understand the stock, than understanding the dog! Whether you decide to teach your dog commands before or after proper 'work' is commenced, it is advisable to get a clear idea of what commands you are going to use.

John uses "Come Bye" to go to the left, and "Way T'me" to go to the right. These are Scottish commands, and used almost universally throughout the UK, and also common in the US and Canada. It is not strictly true to say that these are commands to go left or right. "Come Bye" means to go round clockwise in a complete circle; and "Way T'me" to circle in an anti-clockwise direction. This means that only two commands are necessary to place the dog in any position. In order to get the dog to move from that position, John says "Walk On".

The essential command is to stop, and should certainly have been taught before an ACD is introduced to stock. John says "Down" or "Stand", and also uses a whistle for this command. A dog does not always hear a verbal command when working, especially when working cattle, and is much more likely to hear a whistle. For the 'down', John uses a long, shrill note which can be continued until the dog lies down, and a short, sharp 'peep' for the 'stand'. Of course, all commands can be given by whistle – but that depends on how good a whistler you are – and it is important to use commands which come easily, without having to think what sound to make.

When starting a young ACD, John says "Shh" in an exciting tone to encourage the dog to run, but he usually drops it once the dog knows his sides. When John wants the dog to 'Heel', he hisses "Sst". In fact, we use that sound to encourage a dog to have a go at anything. Apart from that, the only other command John uses is "Steady" in varying tones, which means exactly what it says. Americans usually say "Easy" which means exactly the same. It does not matter at all what commands you use. What does matter is that the dog knows what they mean. This will only happen if the same command is always used for each action .

THE RIGHT START

Once a dog has been taught to drive away, it is usually very difficult, if not impossible to get the dog to gather. On the other hand, a dog which gathers and fetches stock can usually be taught to drive away quite easily. For that reason, John never lets a dog drive away until he can rely on that dog to gather and keep stock right up to him. For those who want an ACD to fetch stock, it is advisable to adopt this principle. Those who only want their ACD to drive stock away from them, can ignore it.

Do not start a young dog in a wide open space, or you may see both stock and dog disappearing over the horizon! Always start in quite a small, enclosed space where you can get at the dog if things go wrong. Do not start on animals that are likely to be awkward and challenge a young dog. By nature, sheep, the hunted animal, will instinctively run from a dog, the hunter. But sheep are often kept under unnatural conditions, and tame sheep may either ignore or challenge a dog. When that happens, the dog has one of two options – run away, or retaliate, neither of which will do much good.

CORRECTION

If your ACD has never met stock before, it may be advisable to put your dog on a line – especially if the stock belong to someone else! Some young dogs are a bit over-enthusiastic with their teeth. By now, your dog should understand that "No" or "Agh!" means "Stop doing that immediately – or else!" If your ACD decides to "have a pook", as our Scottish friends would say, you should be able to stop this with a verbal reprimand. But if the dog really grabs hold of a sheep, you will have to correct quite severely with a hefty yank on the line, at the same time berating the dog harshly.

Correction should be in proportion to the dog's keenness to work, which depends on the strength of the individual's herding instinct. While a dog has to be corrected for biting, care should be taken not to over-correct for herding. Actually, most dogs which tend to use their teeth, are keen enough to stand quite a lot of correction. A young dog must also be stopped from rushing in and grabbing the heels of cattle willy-nilly. A stockdog should control stock, but at the same time cause as little harassment or stress as possible.

CONTROL

A line can be very helpful in teaching a dog to drive away or for some other movements; but there would be obvious problems if the dog ran right round a flock with a line attached. If you are really worried about your dog gripping, you could use a muzzle, which is, apparently, done in Australia. We have never done this, but we cannot see that it would do any harm. It could, in fact, be very helpful by allowing you to give lots of encouragement, without worrying that the dog might grip a sheep.

If your dog makes an attempt to grip, you must correct quite severely, so that the dog understands that it is not allowed. If you do use a muzzle, make sure that it is comfortable and that the dog can pant quite easily. The dog should have a chance to get used to wearing a muzzle, before being expected to work in it. Once the dog is under control, you should be able to remove the muzzle.

FIRST EXERCISES

Start in an enclosed area of not more than half an acre, and try to get the sheep as near the centre as possible before sending the dog. John keeps a young dog on a lead until he gets the sheep in a good position, and he usually has a trained dog to help him get them there. If you do not have a trained dog, it may help to have an assistant who should keep the sheep away from the fence before you send the dog.

How near you get to the sheep depends on what sort of sheep you are using, but the nearer you get, the more control you will have, if the dog makes a mistake, which is highly likely. The ACDs that John has trained to work sheep, did have a strong inclination to grip. But he had less difficulty in checking this problem than with many Border Collies that he has trained. The ever-increasing number of ACDs who work sheep in American Stock Dog Trials proves that they can work sheep quite well.

When you have succeeded in getting a small flock of six to ten sheep to settle near the centre of the training area, walk quietly towards them with your ACD on a lead. As you approach, they are likely to move away. That is when to release the dog, at the same time giving an encouraging "Shh". If you are lucky, the dog will run right round the sheep, but the novice is just as likely to

George Hi (Ch. Beronganella Dandy CDX – Ch. Rewuri Tuki), working at the 1992 ACDCA National Specialty. Owned and handled by Larry Painter, bred by Pat Lewis.
Lori Herbel.

scatter them. You will have to stop this, but be careful not to correct too harshly, or your ACD will think he must not go near the sheep. Better a dog that does the wrong thing, than a dog that does nothing. At this stage you have only one thing in mind – getting the dog to go to the other side of the sheep.

Some dogs will stay at the opposite side of their own accord. Others will run round and round the flock, passing between the handler and the sheep on the way. Some will go halfway round and then come back to the handler, others will go right round and return to the handler on the other side. The sheep are unlikely to stand there like statues, so it is really impossible to say what will happen. Your ACD may not even be interested in the sheep; in his case, you could encourage the dog by "shooing" the sheep away.

Alternatively, the youngster might run with another dog, which is not always a good idea. The other dog must be completely under control. Dogs can learn a lot from other dogs – but rarely anything their owner wants them to learn! It may be that your dog's herding instinct has not yet developed, and you will have to wait a bit longer. A dog can be taught how to herd, but only if the instinct is there in the first place.

HEADING
If your ACD heads the sheep, and then looks as though he is going to come back to you, give the command to drop. If the sheep take this opportunity to move off, try to get the dog to head them, and then give the command to drop when the dog gets to the other side. If the sheep stay fairly still, place yourself directly opposite the dog, move backwards and tell the dog to "walk on". The dog will not understand the command, but if you encourage by tone of voice, the dog should, at least, move towards the sheep, which should make them move towards you.

If you have fairly tame sheep, which will follow you for food, this can be helpful in the early stages, but they should not be so tame that they will face the dog. If the sheep move to one side or the other, the dog should instinctively head them, to keep them coming towards you. If your ACD fails to do this, move yourself, so that the dog is always opposite you. The aim is to encourage the herding instinct until the dog will, of his own accord, keep the sheep moving towards you.

Do not use too many commands at this stage. Just "Shh" to go out and the occasional "Good Boy" in an encouraging tone, to let the dog know that he is doing the right thing. If your ACD gets too close say "Steady" in a steady tone, and if that does not work, give the command to drop. This will give the sheep a chance to move away, and you then call the dog on again. Keep walking backwards, so that you can keep a constant eye on the dog. Or perhaps, more important, so that the dog sees that you have an eye on him!

Soon, very soon, if you have an ACD with a strong herding instinct, you should be able to walk round in different directions, with the dog 'wearing' the sheep behind you, without any instructions at all – but still keep an eye on your dog! This should strengthen the herding instinct and, at the same time, develop a habit of keeping the stock together. It will also encourage the dog to use his own initiative – rather like Kaleski's dog bringing 1000 head of cattle behind him on a dark night!

GATHERING

A dog that will only gather and keep stock to the handler will not do a lot of good in trials, but such a dog will be of some real practical use. If you want to move stock from one place to another, all you have to do is walk ahead, open gates and let the dog do the rest. This sort of dog can be expected to do the right thing in an emergency. If you are loading or unloading stock on a dark night and one breaks away, you are unlikely to know where it has gone. But the dog knows, and if the habit of heading and fetching has been developed, that dog can be relied on to bring the animal back to you while you attend to the others. You cannot give instructions, because you do not know where the runaway is, and in an emergency – which often means panic – you may not give very clear instructions anyhow. Our experience suggests that, when in doubt, a dog taught to drive away before being taught to fetch will almost invariably chase stock away.

TEACHING SIDES

Once your ACD will keep the sheep up to you, you can start to teach the dog sides. If you move to the left, the sheep should move to the right. The dog, being accustomed to keeping them to you, is likely to head them without being told. If, as you prepare to move to the left, you give the command "Come Bye," the dog should soon learn to move before the sheep have moved. Then give the command "Way T'me," move to your right, and the dog should move anti-clockwise.

As soon as your ACD can be relied on to run round the sheep from a short distance and bring them to you, it is time to increase the distance you send the dog. The ACD is a close run, loose-eyed dog, and the problem you are most likely to have had, so far, is that your dog keeps too close to the sheep. When you extend the distance you send the dog, the most likely response is for the dog to run straight towards the sheep. As the sheep see the dog approaching, they will run away, which will really excite the dog, so that he will probably rush close past the sheep and turn them back to you. Better than running after sheep yourself, but not at all likely to put weight on the sheep! It is unlikely that an ACD will cast out like a Border Collie, but you should be able to improve the outrun. You can prevent it getting worse, which will certainly happen if you allow the dog to persist in this way. Make the dog lie down and place yourself between the dog and the sheep. Give the command "Come Bye", and go with your dog to the left. If the dog rushes towards the sheep, give the command to drop, go up to the dog, and repeat the whole procedure, making the dog go out again. Do the same the other way, with the command "Way T'me". In this way, you are teaching the dog to keep back from the sheep on the outrun, and at the same time reinforcing the right and left commands.

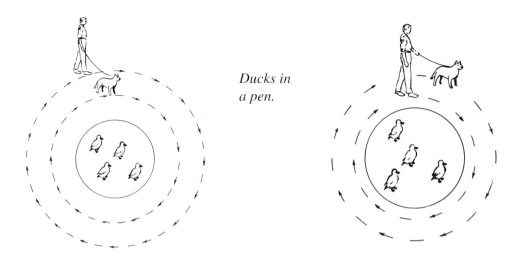

Ducks in a pen.

THE PEN

In his book, *The Farmer's Dog*, John explains how to teach various commands with a few ducks in a pen of about 6ft square, or a round one of about the same size. Sheep or calves can be used, and the great advantage is that the animals are not harassed. Sheep, and even more so ducks, will tire much more quickly than a dog. When they are confined in a pen, you can keep on until the dog gets the message, rather than having to give up when the stock show signs of exhaustion. A dog can be taught all the commands by this method. If you put a line on the dog, you can correct as and when mistakes occur. With the aid of a line you can stop the dog rushing about, and reinforce the lesson of walking quietly.

Give the commands "Come Bye" and "Way T'me", as described above, and go round the pen in either direction, with the dog slightly ahead of you. Note that you are following the dog, not leading the dog. If your ACD comes too close to the pen, correct with a jerk on the line. Alternate this by having the dog between yourself and the pen. But do not simply hold the dog back from the pen. Have the line slack, but be ready to correct if the dog goes too close. Take the dog away from the pen, command "Walk on", "Stand", "Come Bye", "Come here", and so on, with each and every command, until they really become fixed in the dog's mind. With the line you are able to apply instant correction if the dog disobeys.

THE WHISTLE

Teach the dog to stop to a whistle, as well as a verbal command. If you cannot whistle with your fingers, there are lots of whistles on the market. A high-pitched, shrill whistle is best. We do not care for 'silent' whistles; We have known several dogs which hated them – the ultra-sonic sound seemed to hurt their ears. Besides, it is helpful to the handler to hear the noise they are making! By giving a long blast, followed immediately by "Down", or a short 'peep' followed by "Stand", the dog should soon stop to the whistle in anticipation of the verbal command.

Once the dog obeys all the commands on a line, you can remove the line, and the dog should obey just as well without. If your dog is reluctant to obey one or two commands, put the line back on and concentrate on these. Several people have tried and approved this method, or modified versions of it, and it is recommended by at least one very famous sheepdog trainer. John's

The art of driving displayed by Ch. Buzzards Rapped In Class (Ch. Buzzards Red Tubs – Buzzards Blue Fox), owned by Doug and Tracy Carlton.

Lori Herbel.

reservations arise from the fact that these people all use Border Collies. Not all ACDs would be keen enough – or stupid enough, depending on how you look at it – to keep on 'working' stock that is not going anywhere, and quite obviously cannot go anywhere! But it is certainly the easiest way to teach a dog all the commands, both from the handler's and the animal's point of view.

DRIVING EXERCISES

So far we have been concentrating on teaching the dog to bring stock to the handler. For practical purposes, it is helpful if the dog will move stock in various directions, and for herding trials it is essential. This is why it is important to spend time teaching your ACD all the different directional commands. Once the dog knows these, and more importantly obeys them, there should be fewer problems.

You should now have a dog which will keep the sheep up to you without any commands, that will circle the flock in either direction, and will pass between the sheep and the handler. If you want to drive away, send the dog to either side with "Come Bye" or "Way T'me", and give the command to drop before the dog starts to head; now give "Come Here", and as the dog approaches you, give the command to go to the other side, and then stop the dog again. The sheep should now be moving away from you, but they are still in the same position in relation to the dog as they were before. It is you who have changed position, and the dog should still answer the same commands.

Move forward with the dog to begin with, but reduce your pace until you are standing still, so that the dog is driving the sheep away from you. Alternate this by walking to the side of the sheep, and making the dog go away from you and come back to you, behind them. It may help to have the sheep alongside a fence, which will reduce the temptation for the dog to run right round them. Again, you can drop back and let the dog drive the sheep on his own. You can also change direction by making the dog head the sheep, and then take them back the way they have come.

From there, you can stand in the middle of the field and make the dog drive the sheep round you in a big circle. Be sure to make your ACD drive in both directions. If one side is favoured more than the other, work the dog mostly to the 'bad' side, until your ACD runs equally well to both sides. As the dog is not going to run round the sheep, you can use a line on all these driving exercises. Of course, under working conditions you would go with the dog and help to drive the stock. But in trials a dog has to move stock in various directions, and this can often be a great help round the farm too.

WORKING CATTLE

The reason sheep run away when they see a dog is not because they are stupid, as some stupid people believe. Anyone who understands sheep knows that they are far from stupid. The reason they run from a dog is because, by nature, a sheep is a hunted animal and the dog is a hunter. When a hunter appears, a hunted animal either flees or stands its ground and fights, depending on which tactic offers the better chance of survival. Although often smaller than a sheep, a dog the size of an ACD or Border Collie can kill a sheep, and has frequently done so. But a dog of that size could not kill a cow, so the best chance of survival here is for the cow to stand its ground and fight.

If a stray dog enters a field where sheep are grazing, the flock will almost certainly take off to the far side of the field. In contrast, if a dog goes into a field with cattle which are not accustomed to a dog, it is pretty certain they will rush towards the dog, gather round and even attack it. The chance of this happening is much greater if the cattle are cows with suckled calves at foot. Quite near where we live, a lady, tragically, was recently trampled to death by a herd of cows with calves at foot, when she was attempting to rescue her Pekingese. Ironically, the dog escaped injury.

Cattle will not instinctively move away from a dog, as sheep do, but although they are not very clever, they can easily be taught to do so by a good dog. Cattle learn by the same principle as the dog has learned – correction and reward. If a beast breaks away from the herd or refuses to go forward, it gets bitten. If it stays with the others and moves in the right direction, it doesn't get bitten. Not exactly reward, but certainly more pleasant than being bitten by a dog!

Do not worry that your ACD will not heel cattle because you have stopped your dog from biting sheep. A dog's reactions to sheep and cattle are quite different, and we have known many dogs that would tackle cattle with enthusiasm, but would not touch a sheep. However, a dog can't be taught to heel – at least we have never heard of any way that it can be taught. The trait can be encouraged, but if a dog will not heel, it will not heel. This is unlikely to render the dog useless as a worker but, depending on the sort of stock to be worked, the dog will be a good deal less efficient. In fact, this problem is very unlikely to occur in the ACD; the breed has a very strong heeling instinct, even when not worked for several generations.

Whether you have started your dog on sheep or are starting straight on to cattle, it is important to start with stock that moves freely. In an effort to build up confidence, a young dog should feel in charge. The relationship between the dog and the stock should be similar to that between you and your dog. Your dog will do what you command without being afraid of you. Likewise, cattle accustomed to being worked by a good dog, will do what the dog wants them to, without being frightened.Cattle unaccustomed to being 'dogged' tend to rush about wildly and split in all directions. The young dog doesn't know what to do in such a situation, and in an effort to cope, may well make matters worse. Once the dog has learned that cattle will move in the direction he wants, the dog should gain confidence which, in turn, should give the cattle confidence.

Some people recommend starting a young dog on calves, but we once saw a six-month-old calf badly lamed by a young ACD. Cattle which come to feed, or dairy cows that go to be milked, can be useful in the early stages. They know where they are going, you know where they are going, and it is easy to make the dog believe that he is taking them there. Young stock are less likely to face a dog than older animals and, of course, a kick from a yearling is less likely to discourage a young dog than a kick from a three-year-old.

Note how low to the ground the ACD is, before biting, showing a different style to the dog on page 152.

HEELING

Just as you cannot teach a dog to Heel, neither can you teach a dog *how* to Heel. That is something the dog will have to learn, partly by instinct and partly from experience. There must be few working Cattle Dogs that have not been kicked in their youth. A well-aimed blow to the jaw from an adult animal can put a young dog off, sometimes for life. A few glancing blows or near misses should teach a dog how to avoid them. The best dogs usually bite low down on the heel, and are least likely to be kicked.

However, a dog does not bite and then lie down to avoid being kicked, as some books tell us. The low heeler is usually on his elbows and has his brisket on the ground before he bites. The dog keeps his head down until the hoof passes over it, but his hindquarters rarely touch the ground. Some dogs swerve sideways rather like a boxer who delivers a blow, and then swerves to avoid one in return. Some dogs bite above the heel, and some bite the hock, which is not at all a good idea as the dog is very liable to be kicked and the stock lamed.

When heading, a dog may bite a beast by the nose, the cheek or the front foot. Some will bite the nose or the cheek, and immediately reinforce the lesson by biting the front foot. We have never seen any of the Collie types do this, but it is quite common among ACDs. Kulta, our own ACD, always grabbed the cheek, which seemed to be more effective than 'nosing', because the beast quickly turns its head away from the dog, and is immediately heading in the right direction.

As the beast turns, the dog is presented with an opportunity to nip the heel and send the animal on its way back amongst the others. This is what should happen, but some dogs stick to the beast's head and keep turning it round and round in circles. This is an abomination which can, and often does become a habit. Like all habits it should be quickly, and severely nipped in the bud. At this stage, you should still be working in the enclosed arena, as with the sheep, and if your dog shows an inclination to do this, make sure this habit is corrected, before you go out into wide, open spaces. There are few certainties in training, but one of the few is that, if a dog cannot be controlled in a confined area, that dog will not be controlled in open country.

It is really a question of Obedience. As the beast turns away from the dog, give the command to Drop. This may be easier said than done. The average dog will be excited and unlikely to hear you. A whistle is better than shouting, and you can keep up a long blast on the whistle until the dog does hear and lies down. This should allow the beast to move away from the dog, and you can either give a "Sst" to send the animal on its way, or send the dog round to gather the others.

The AKC rules for Herding Trials quite rightly stipulate that unnecessary biting will be penalised. When driving a big mob of cattle, a good dog will work back and forward behind them, having a nip at a few heels while passing. The dog is not told when to Heel, and the beast that is nipped will crush in amongst the others where it is unlikely to be bitten again for some time. With a small group of animals the situation is very different. We have seen a dog quietly walking behind five steers at a trial, when he was told by his handler to heel. The bitten animal took off like a rocket, quickly followed by the other four. The dog got over-excited and the whole thing ended in chaos.

Whether you intend competing in trials, or just keeping a few animals on a small farm, it is important that your dog does not bite unless it is necessary. The ACDs we have known have all been prone to having a sly nip, if they thought they could get away with it; it is important not to let this become a habit.

Essential as training is, it is not really a substitute for work, and few of us have the time or facilities to give our dogs the amount of work they need. Training therefore becomes even more essential. This includes training for any purpose – Obedience, Agility, Flyball – or anything else that will exercise the dog's mind and body. A dog, well-exercised behind a horse or bike, will be a lot easier to train than one which only gets a half-hour's walk each day. And in the show ring, that dog will have a lot more of that hard, muscular condition the Standard calls for.

Chapter Twelve

BREEDING

The first question to ask yourself is, "Why do I want to breed?" If you want another dog exactly like the one you already have, well, you are very *unlikely* to get it. You will have better odds betting on horses than the whelping box! Perhaps you think that breeding will make you money? Forget that one. You may think it will be fun to have a litter of pups. Maybe it will, but it will also be hard work, time-consuming, messy and expensive. It may be that you think your ACD is such a good specimen, she ought to be bred from. First check your own opinion with an experienced breeder; you might find your swan is really a goose.

Perhaps you are a serious ACD owner, and you are really interested in the breed. You have a good sort of bitch, healthy, sound and with a good temperament, and a pedigree with the right sort of dogs going back for several generations. You know several people who would genuinely like a puppy, and you want to keep one yourself. The breeder agrees that she could produce a good offspring. Then OK, but have a long hard think about it; do some research, and if you finally decide to go ahead, do so with caution.

THE STUD DOG

The first thing is to find a suitable stud dog, and this will entail deciding on the type of breeding programme you wish to pursue. These fall into three basic categories:

LINE BREEDING: The mating of related dogs such as grandam to grandson, or niece to uncle. If the dog and bitch share one or more ancestors in the first three generations, that falls under the category of line breeding.

IN BREEDING: This is mating two *VERY CLOSELY* related dogs, such as mother and son, and *it is not to be undertaken by novices,* as it can introduce weaknesses into a line.

OUTCROSSING: This is what it says – the mating of two apparently unrelated dogs.

Do not rush out and pick a stud dog because he excels in the qualities your bitch lacks. Consult someone who has experience of the breed, preferably the breeder of your bitch, who will know what type of breeding will suit her. Make sure that any dog you are considering using is free from hereditary defects. Go to dog shows, herding trials, Obedience trials etc., and take a good look at the dogs there. Talk to the owners and see for yourself the type of stock the dog is producing. If you decide to bring a litter of ACD pups into the world, it is your responsibility to ensure that they are a credit to the breed and a pleasure to their new owners.

THE BROOD BITCH

Having chosen your stud dog, make sure your bitch is fit and not fat. Fat bitches are notoriously

Aust. Ch. Landmaster Darling Red 1978 (Aust. Ch. Landmaster U'Sundowner – Rocambole Red Jody), with two of her sons. 'Honey' was an outstanding brood bitch, producing ten Championship Show winners in three litters.

Sally Anne Thompson.

difficult to get in whelp, and if they become pregnant, they often have difficulty whelping. If you have not bred a litter before it would be a good idea to have your bitch checked over by a vet. Make sure you take his advice about worming.

Most bitches come in season twice a year, but do not mate your bitch at her first season. First signs are often frequent urination, swelling of the vulva, and a bloody discharge – not to mention the interest of the neighbourhood dogs. A season normally lasts three weeks. However, many bitches do not seem to know this! Some have very short seasons of only two weeks, others may stay in season for up to five weeks.

Nearly every book tells you that your bitch will be ready for mating between ten and twelve days – do not believe it. We have known bitches ready to mate at seven days, and others who will fly at any dog for nearly three weeks, and then stand happily to be mated on the twenty-first day. In our experience ACD bitches are generally ready for mating later, rather than earlier, in the season.

In the case of a difficult bitch it is now possible to test for the optimum time to mate. A vet will be able to take a series of blood tests so that progesterone peak at ovulation can be seen. Usually a bitch will be ready for mating when the bloody discharge becomes paler, and the slightest pressure on her rump causes her to stand still cocking her tail to one side. An experienced stud dog will be able to tell you in no uncertain manner when she is ready!

If possible, arrange to have two matings, as that is far more satisfactory than one, especially in a maiden bitch. Once mated, remember to keep the bitch away from other dogs until she has completely finished her season.

ARTIFICIAL INSEMINATION (AI)

This is especially relevant for breeders in the UK and other European countries where the gene pool is small. There have recently been great improvements in the technology in providing chilled or frozen semen for AI. The prospects for a successful insemination have also improved. A number of American companies have developed a system to collect, ship and store fresh chilled or frozen semen (a list can be obtained from the AKC). Of special interest to ACD breeders is the fact that they have set up four freezing centres in Australia.

THE IN-WHELP BITCH

Few bitches show signs of being in whelp until around the fourth week, after which time you can sometimes feel the pups. If you want to know for sure if the bitch is in whelp, and how many pups she will have, you can now have a scan done by a vet. This is an ultrasound imaging system, designed for pregnancy detection and foetal numbering.

The in-whelp bitch will need plenty of exercise and good food. Assuming that you are feeding a complete diet recommended for bitches in whelp, or a homemade diet with the necessary additions, she will not need any extra food for the first few weeks. If the total food allowance is increased by ten per cent each week from six weeks onwards, she will be getting about fifty per cent more food by the time she is due to whelp, and this should prove satisfactory.

By that time she should also have a tummy full of pups, and she will need her feed divided between two or three smaller feeds. As already said, if you are feeding a balanced diet, she should not need any extras. If the bitch is carrying a large litter, she may become less eager to exercise during the last few weeks, but should be encouraged to take regular, steady exercise. Having said that, most of our bitches charge about in the forest until the day they whelp, but I am not saying that we recommend this!

A week or so before she is due to whelp, introduce the bitch to the whelping box and let her sleep in it at night. This should be in a quiet, warm place, and large enough for her to lie comfortably on her side.

Most pregnancies last from fifty-eight to sixty-eight days, sixty-three days being the norm. At the time of whelping, make sure the room is warm; nothing kills newborn puppies more quickly than cold. We have found that the best type of bedding is a synthetic sheepskin, which allows moisture to drain through. Place this over a thick layer of newspaper, and you will have a warm, dry, comfortable bed, which can be changed when necessary and easily washed.

THE WHELPING

When she gets near whelping, a bitch may appear worried, restless, pant, dig up her bed, and probably start shivering or trembling. This may go on for several hours. At this stage, take her temperature, as it will drop – possibly as low as 98F – near the onset of labour. Try not to fuss. If the bitch is managing all right, watch her, but do not interfere unless you are needed.

When the first pup appears, it will be enclosed in a sac which the bitch normally tears open, and then she bites through the umbilical cord. She will then most likely eat the afterbirth. Some breeders are against this, but we usually let our bitches eat two or three, and then take the rest away, as too many can cause diarrhoea.

The bitch will usually lick the puppy dry, but if she is busy delivering another, you may have to do this for her by giving the pup a good rub with a rough towel. If the bitch has not bitten off the cord, you will need to have some sterilised cotton ready, and tie it about one inch from the body wall and cut it the other side of the tie.

The interval between the delivery of the pups can vary from fifteen minutes to several hours. If the bitch is relaxed and resting between deliveries, all is well. But intermittent, prolonged labour is another thing. If a bitch labours for two or three hours, and no pups appear, it is time to call your vet. You should also call the vet if the head of a puppy appears but the pup is not delivered within about fifteen minutes.

It is not always easy to tell if a bitch has finished whelping, and so it is a good idea to get your vet to check her over to make sure. When she has finished, take her out to relieve herself; you will need a lead, as she will not want to leave her new pups. You can use this time to give her a clean bed, and when she returns, give her a drink of milk and honey, and leave her to rest quietly. It is important to leave some fresh water available, as she will be thirsty after all that effort.

POST-WHELPING

For the first day or so, keep the bitch on a light diet, after which she will need a greatly increased amount of food. A bitch with a large litter will need up to four times the normal maintenance allowance. Make sure you are feeding a suitable diet for lactating bitches, and feed her several times a day. For the first few days the bitch may not want to leave the pups, but she should be taken out at intervals, which are gradually increased.

After about ten days, the puppies will start to open their eyes and begin to move about more freely. This is the time you should clip their nails. Just nip off the tips with an ordinary pair of nail scissors. If you neglect to do this, the pups will scratch the bitch and make her quite sore. She may then be very disinclined to let them feed. You will need to continue clipping their nails until they are weaned. You will also need to worm the litter (see Chapter Nine: Caring for your ACD). You should also make sure that the bitch can get away from the pups when she wants – a bench that she can jump on to is a good idea.

WEANING

At three weeks we start to wean our pups by giving them their first meal. We used to start them on scraped raw meat and goat's milk, but we now use a good brand of complete puppy food and puppy milk, and the pups seem to thrive on this.

Start with one meal, gradually increasing to four by the time the puppies are five weeks old. Some bitches regurgitate their food for the pups. This is quite normal behaviour, but it is not very helpful to you. So when you feed the bitch, keep her away from the pups for a while. Once the pups are feeding well, start to decrease the amount of food you give the bitch, and increase her exercise. This will help to dry up the milk. By the time they are five weeks old she should be spending most of the day away from them, and at six weeks the litter should be completely weaned.

Eclampsia, or Milk Fever, is something that you should be on the look out for. If this is going to occur it usually does so between two and three weeks after whelping. The bitch will become restless, breathe rapidly, possibly have staggering fits, tremble, or yap consistently. It cannot be emphasised enough that this is an emergency, and you should call your vet *at once*. A calcium injection usually results in a rapid recovery.

PUPPY REARING

Right from the start, handle the pups as much as possible. The more human contact they have, the better. Do not be afraid to make a noise: ACD pups are tough little characters, and the sooner they find out what a noisy place the world is, the better. Very young pups take little interest in anything

Puppies come rushing when food is on offer, and this can be combined with teaching them to come when called.   *Sally Anne Thompson.*

except milk and sleep, but it will do no harm to pick them up for a cuddle. Newborn pups should be quiet, with just the occasional squeak. If they are restless and noisy, check that they are neither too hot nor too cold. Although they need to be kept warm, they do not want to be treated as hot-house plants!

Once their eyes are open, at about ten days, the pups soon become far more adventurous and want to explore beyond their box. They should be given the opportunity to do this, and should also be given toys to play with. Be careful not to let them have anything harmful, which could be swallowed or stick in their throats. Nylabones, solid rubber balls, rope-tugs are all suitable items. Once they get to this stage, put down newspaper outside their box, and, with any luck, you should find that they will soon run out to relieve themselves .ACD pups develop more quickly than most other breeds. From about four weeks onwards, you can start introducing them to different sights and sounds. Bring them in the house, take them out into the garden, either as a pack or individually. Invite friends to come and see them. If you have children of your own, let them play together. If you have no children, borrow some, but make sure they are 'biddable'!

Get the puppies used to grooming. There is not much to do at this stage, but you can stand them on a table, one at a time, and teach them to be still while you run your hands over them and give them a brush. By six weeks old, all the pups should have become used to being on a collar and lead. This does not mean you should teach them heelwork; just accustom them to having a short walk. They should also be taken for short car journeys. All this will make life much easier for them in the new home, and easier for their new owner too. If at all possible, have the whole litter BAER tested for deafness before they are sold.

It is now generally accepted that pups should go to their new homes at six or seven weeks. If some have to stay on a little longer, it is vital that you keep them socialised – never leave them isolated in a kennel, cut off from the outside world.